SMARTSUITE
in easy steps

Stephen Copestake

COMPUTER
STEP

In easy steps is an imprint of Computer Step
Southfield Road . Southam
Warwickshire CV33 OFB . England

Tel: 01926 817999 Fax: 01926 817005
http://www.computerstep.com

Reprinted 1999
Third edition 1998
Second edition 1997
First published 1996

Notice of Liability

Every effort has been made to ensure that this book contains accurate
and current information. However, Computer Step and the author shall
not be liable for any loss or damage suffered by readers as a result of
any information contained herein.

Trademarks

SmartSuite, Word Pro, 1-2-3, Approach and Freelance Graphics are
registered trademarks of Lotus Development Corporation. Microsoft
and Windows are registered trademarks of Microsoft Corporation. All
other trademarks are acknowledged as belonging to their respective
companies.

Printed and bound in the United Kingdom

ISBN 1-84078-013-4

Contents

3 1-2-3   91

4 Approach   123

5   Freelance Graphics   155

6   Organizer   179

Index   187

First steps

Chapter One

This chapter shows you how SmartSuite provides a common look, so you can get started quickly in most of the modules. You'll learn how to create new documents and open/save existing ones, locally and on the Internet. You'll also discover how to use SmartMasters to create more detailed documents. You'll use SmartCenter to (among other things) directly access useful Web sites. Finally, you'll create your own with FastSite.

Covers

Introduction

Lotus SmartSuite consists of six principal modules:

- Word Pro (word processor);

- 1-2-3 (spreadsheet);

- Approach (database);

- Freelance Graphics (slide show creator);

- Organizer (contact and task manager), and;

- FastSite (tool for converting/publishing Web files).

FastSite – only available in the Millennium edition – has its own look and feel.

The first five modules provide a high level of functionality and ease of use. Another advantage is that, with the exception of FastSite, they're well integrated. To a large extent, they share a common look and feel.

The illustration below shows the Word Pro opening screen. Flagged are components which are common to most of the other modules, too.

Millennium Edition users – if ViaVoice is installed, the Word Pro screen is slightly different. See Chapter Two.

SmartIcons provide instant access to commonly used SmartSuite features. Available SmartIcons vary slightly from module to module.

Title bar   Menu bar

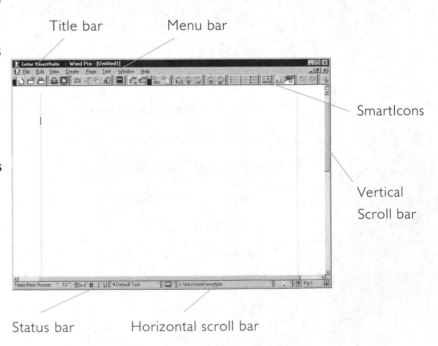

SmartIcons

Vertical Scroll bar

Status bar   Horizontal scroll bar

...cont'd

In SmartSuite 97, these screens look slightly different.

Notice the screen components that are held in common. The purpose of this shared approach is to ensure that users of SmartSuite can move between modules with the minimum of readjustment.

There are, of course, differences between the module screens; we'll explore these in later sections.

The Organizer and FastSite screens are rather different – see Chapter Six and pages 34–40 respectively.

Compare this with the following:

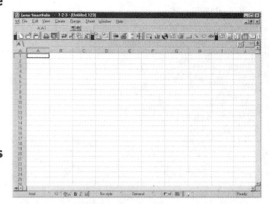

1-2-3 screen

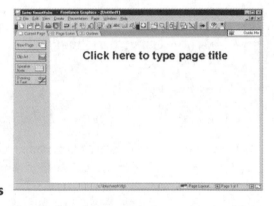

Click here to type page title

Freelance Graphics screen

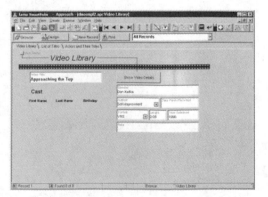

Approach screen

SmartIcons

'Cycling' is a feature unique to SmartSuite. When you click a Cycle button repeatedly, SmartSuite steps through associated options automatically until the correct one is activated.

In Freelance Graphics and Approach, pull down the View menu and click Show SmartIcons. Repeat to hide SmartIcons.
In 1-2-3, click Hide SmartIcons in the View menu. Click Show SmartIcons to reverse the operation.
In FastSite, click Show, Icon bar in the View menu. Repeat to reverse.
In Organizer, press F11 to hide all extraneous screen components. Repeat to reverse.

All the principal SmartSuite modules provide access to a variety of SmartIcons. These are buttons you can click to initiate editing actions, and are contained in an on-screen bar which varies according to module. SmartIcons symbolise and allow easy access to often-used commands which would normally have to be invoked via one or more menus.

For example, Word Pro's default SmartIcon bar lets you:

• create, open, save and print documents;

• launch Infoboxes (see later in this chapter);

• cycle through alignment and/or indent options;

• cycle through typeface and/or type size options;

• cycle through text attribute options (bold, italic and underline), and;

• spell-check text

by simply clicking on the relevant button.

Hiding/revealing SmartIcons – the menu route
In Word Pro, pull down the View menu. Do the following:

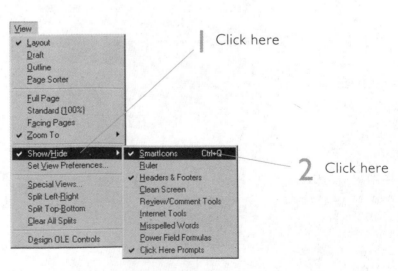

Click here

2 Click here

...cont'd

Hiding/revealing SmartIcons – an alternative

You can use another, and more versatile, method to control which SmartIcon sets (bars) display. (Just about any editing operation you can perform from within SmartSuite menus can be incorporated as a SmartIcon, for ease of access.) Using this method, you can hide a specific set, or all sets.

In any module apart from FastSite, do the following:

Click any SmartIcon command button, as here

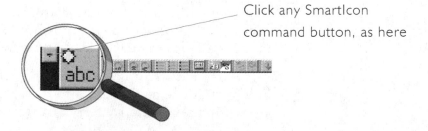

Now do either of the following:

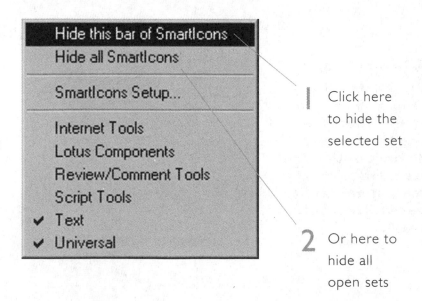

The **options here vary according** to the module you're currently using.

1 Click here to hide the selected set

2 Or here to hide all open sets

Customising SmartIcons

You can:

- specify which bar displays;

- add buttons to existing SmartIcon bars;

- remove buttons from bars, and;

- specify button size.

In any module apart from FastSite, click a SmartIcon command button (see page 11 for how to do this). In the menu that appears, click SmartIcons Setup.

Now carry out step 1 below to specify which bar displays. Follow step 2 to add a button to the bar, or step 3 to remove an existing one. Finally, carry out step 4.

3 Click a button; drag it off the bar

HANDY TIP

To adjust the size of SmartIcon buttons, click the arrow to the right of the Icon size field; select the size you want from the list. Then follow step 4.

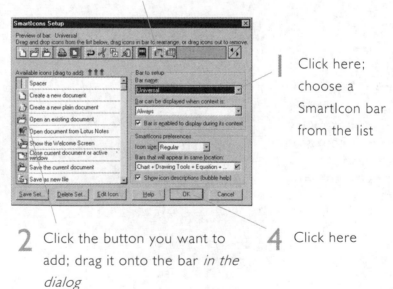

| Click here; choose a SmartIcon bar from the list

2 Click the button you want to add; drag it onto the bar *in the dialog*

4 Click here

Infoboxes – an overview

Many of the SmartSuite modules offer a feature which, until recently, had only been seen in top-of-the-range Desktop Publishing packages. You can use *Infoboxes*, collections of linked formatting features (called 'properties' in SmartSuite), to make editing changes on-the-fly.

Below is the Text Properties Infobox from Word Pro:

To activate a different Infobox, click here; select the new Infobox from the list

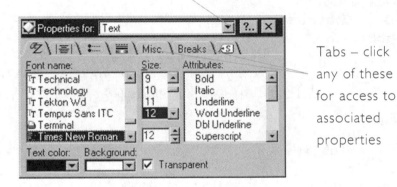

Tabs – click any of these for access to associated properties

Infoboxes provide the following advantages:

- If you want, you can have them stay open on-screen while you work (unlike dialogs, which close when you've finished with them). In this way, you can easily make multiple changes with the minimum of effort.

- You can use standard Windows techniques to move them to new locations on-screen.

- Changes you make within an Infobox are applied automatically, while you watch. (You don't have to click on OK to implement them.)

The following are some of the areas where Infoboxes are useful: text formatting, page layout, working with frames, working with headers/footers, columns and drawings.

Launching Infoboxes

SmartSuite lets you use SmartIcons to launch Infoboxes.

This is an excerpt from the default Freelance Graphics SmartIcon bar; the Infobox icon, however, is identical in both Freelance Graphics and Approach.

Approach and Freelance Graphics

The various modules employ slightly different techniques. In Approach and Freelance Graphics, first select whatever it is you want to change. Then do the following:

Click here to launch the relevant Infobox

Word Pro and 1-2-3

There are no Infoboxes in Organizer and FastSite.

Word Pro and 1-2-3, on the other hand, use a more individualistic approach. For examples of this, look at the SmartIcon section below:

SmartIcon which launches the Range Infobox

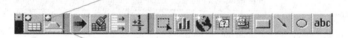

SmartIcon which launches the Sheet Infobox

This example is the icon which launches the Text Properties Infobox from Word Pro. It's used to change typographical features.

The point here is that Word Pro and 1-2-3 provide a variety of *specific* Infobox icons. Each contains a yellow star on a grey background.

Yellow star

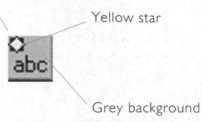

Grey background

New document creation

All SmartSuite modules let you:

- (with the exception of FastSite) create new blank documents, and;

- (with the exception of FastSite and Organizer) create new documents based on automated templates called SmartMasters.

Creating blank documents is the simplest route to new document creation; use this if you want to define the document components yourself from scratch. This is often not the most efficient way to create new documents.

SmartMasters are special templates (document models containing pre-assigned formatting and/or text) which provide a shortcut to the creation of new documents. When activated, SmartMasters contain special 'click here' blocks which tell you where to insert relevant text. SmartMasters greatly simplify and speed up the creation of new documents with highly professional results.

Because the SmartSuite modules (apart from FastSite) are reasonably uniform in the way they create new documents, we'll look at this topic here rather than in later module-specific sections.

Documents created with the use of SmartMasters can easily be amended subsequently.

The illustration below shows the Newsletter SmartMaster which comes with Word Pro.

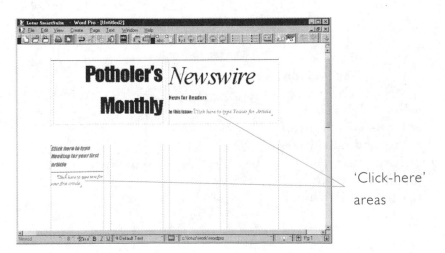

'Click-here' areas

Creating blank documents

You can create a new blank document from within any of the SmartSuite modules (apart from FastSite). However, the procedures are slightly different.

In Word Pro

Pull down the File menu and click New Document. Carry out step 1:

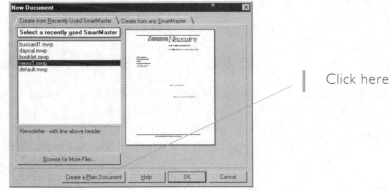

Click here

HANDY TIP

A version of the New dialog (called the 'Welcome' screen) also launches automatically whenever you launch any module apart from Organizer and FastSite.

In Approach

Pull down the File menu and click New Database. Carry out steps 1–2:

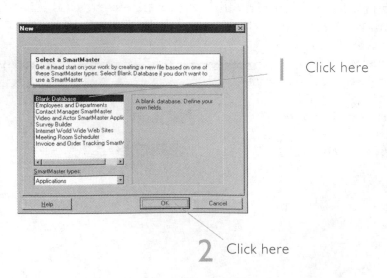

Click here

REMEMBER

In Approach, there are further actions which need to be undertaken before your new database is ready for use – see pages 125–126.

2 Click here

In 1-2-3

Pull down the File menu and click New Workbook. Carry out step 1:

To create a new file in Organizer, simply press Ctrl+N.

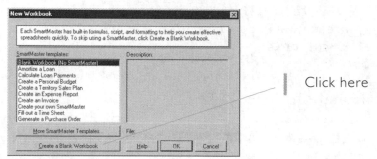

Click here

In Freelance Graphics

Pull down the File menu and click New Presentation. Carry out steps 1–4:

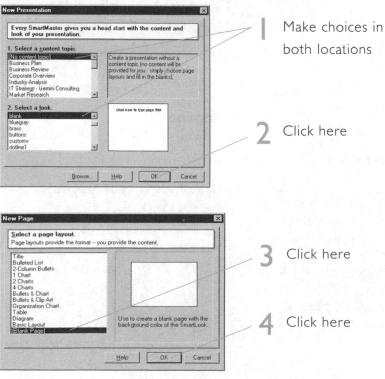

Make choices in both locations

2 Click here

3 Click here

4 Click here

Using SmartMasters

SmartSuite provides a large number of SmartMasters. With these, you can create a wide variety of professional-quality documents. For example, you can create newsletters, business plans and reviews, calendars, business cards, faxes, letters, expense reports, invoices, payment schedules, purchase orders, memos...

For other ways to create new documents based on SmartMasters, see pages 26 and 33.

In Word Pro

Pull down the File menu and click New Document. Perform steps 1-4:

Users of the Millennium edition have access to new Internet-based SmartMasters.

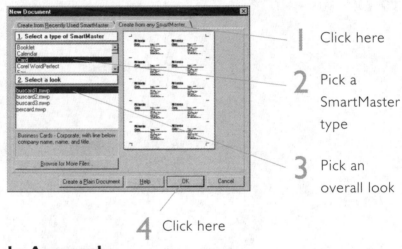

1 Click here

2 Pick a SmartMaster type

3 Pick an overall look

4 Click here

Templates are less complex than SmartMasters.

In Approach

Pull down the File menu and click New Database. Carry out steps 1-2:

To base the new document on a template, click here. Choose Templates in the list. Now follow steps 1 and 2.

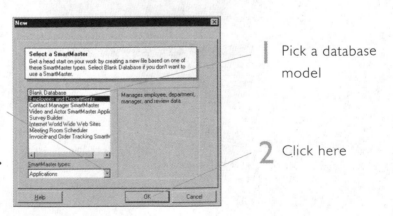

1 Pick a database model

2 Click here

...cont'd

In 1-2-3

Pull down the File menu and click New Workbook. Carry
out steps 1–2:

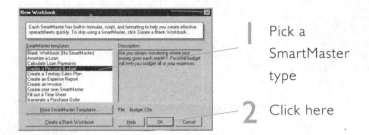

Pick a
SmartMaster
type

Click here

In Freelance Graphics

HANDY TIP

**To create a
new file in
Organizer
(without
the use of
SmartMasters),
press Ctrl+N.**

Pull down the File menu and click New Presentation. Carry
out steps 1–4:

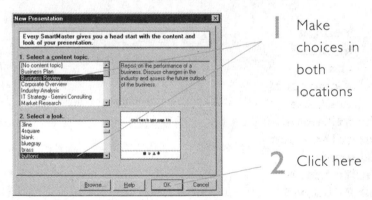

Make
choices in
both
locations

Click here

HANDY TIP

**Content
topics help
you create
effective
slide shows by
suggesting suitable
text and graphics,
when appropriate.**

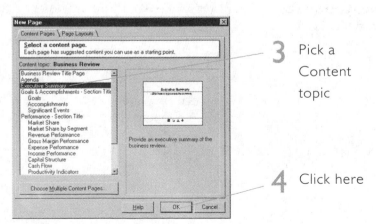

Pick a
Content
topic

Click here

Opening files

You can open Word Pro, 1-2-3, Approach, Freelance Graphics and Organizer documents you've already created.

In any module, pull down the File menu and click Open. Now carry out the following steps, as appropriate:

2 Click here. In the drop-down list, click the drive which hosts the file

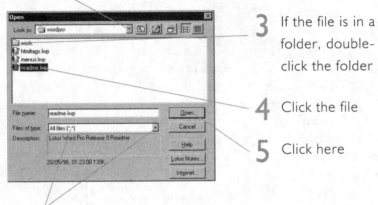

3 If the file is in a folder, double-click the folder

4 Click the file

5 Click here

You can also use the Documents section (available from the Windows Start menu) to open recently used SmartSuite files – see your Windows documentation for how to do this.

1 Make sure the relevant file type is shown. If it isn't, click the arrow and select it from the drop-down list

The Open dialogs for the Word Pro, 1-2-3, Freelance Graphics, Approach and Organizer modules vary slightly. For instance:

• the 'Files of type' field lists differing file formats, and;

• in the 1-2-3 Open dialog, you can opt to open the file on a 'read only' basis (where no amendments to the document can be saved to disk).

Opening files from the Internet

 To open Internet files, you must have a live Internet connection. This means one of the following:

- a modem attached to your PC (plus a live connection to a service provider)
- an ISDN line
- a leased line

In any module apart from Organizer and FastSite, you can open documents directly from the World Wide Web or FTP servers.

First, ensure your Internet connection is open. Launch the relevant Open dialog (see page 20 for how to do this) and click this button:

Then carry out the following steps, as appropriate:

Web connections

Click here

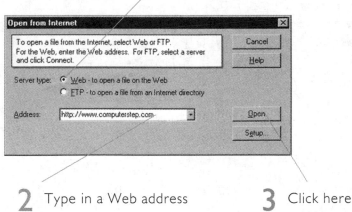

2 Type in a Web address   3 Click here

 Before you open a file on the Internet or a FTP server, you may need to fine-tune your connection settings. To do this, click the Setup button before step 2.
   Complete the dialog which launches – if you need any help doing this (or with any other aspect of connection) consult your service provider or network administrator.

FTP Connections

To open a file from a FTP server, click 'FTP - to open a file from an Internet directory' in step 1. In step 2, select a server. Finally, click this button:

The dialog expands. Select the file you want to open and click:

Saving files

Page 23 shows you how to post files on an Intranet or Internet server. **Word Pro provides a special wizard to help you convert them to HTML format before you do so.**

Pull down the File menu and click Internet, HTML Export Assistant. Complete the dialogs which launch.

Re the above tip – 1-2-3, Freelance Graphics and Approach have similar features.

In 1-2-3 or Freelance Graphics (see page 178), click Internet, Convert to Web Pages in the File menu.

In Approach, click Convert View to Web Pages in the File menu.

Complete the resulting dialogs.

It's important to save your work at frequent intervals, in order to avoid data loss in the event of a hardware fault or power interruption. SmartSuite uses a consistent approach to saving.

Saving a document for the first time

In any of the modules apart from FastSite, pull down the File menu and click Save As. Now do the following:

Click here. In the drop-down list, click the drive you want to host the document

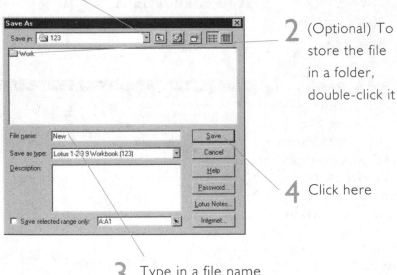

2 (Optional) To store the file in a folder, double-click it

4 Click here

3 Type in a file name

Saving previously saved documents

In any of the modules, pull down the File menu. Now:

*   in Word Pro, Freelance Graphics, 1-2-3 or Organizer, click Save;

*   in Approach, click Save Approach File, and;

*   in FastSite, click Save Sites.

SmartSuite saves the latest version of your document to disk, overwriting the previous one.

Saving files to the Internet

Before you save a file to a FTP server, you need to configure your FTP host settings. To do this, click the Setup button before step 2. Complete the dialog which launches – if you need any help doing this (or with any other aspect of connection) consult your service provider or network administrator.

You can save files in (all modules apart from Organizer) to a FTP server.

In all modules apart from Organizer and FastSite

Ensure your Internet connection is live. Launch the Save As dialog – for how to do this, see page 22. Then do the following:

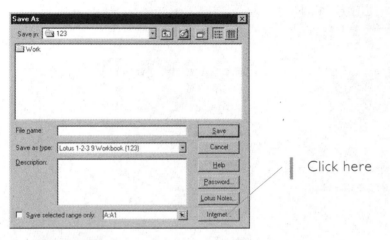

Click here

After step 3, the 'Save to Internet' dialog expands:

Complete this in the normal way. Finally, click Save to save your file to the selected FTP server.

2 Click here; select a server in the list

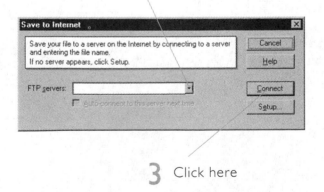

3 Click here

In FastSite

You can use FastSite for batch publishing to the Internet – see page 40.

SmartCenter – an overview

SmartSuite comes with a unique command centre, SmartCenter. Among other things, you can use this to:

- run SmartSuite programs;

- create new documents based on SmartMasters;

- launch a desktop calendar and address book, and;

- connect directly to a variety of Internet sites.

SmartCenter uses a filing cabinet analogy.

Drawers are sub-divided into folders:

The above is an excerpt from the Inernet drawer.

Customising SmartCenter

You can specify where SmartCenter displays. There are two options: at the top or bottom of your screen. You can also arrange to hide it until wanted (by default, it displays on screen continuously). Carry out the following steps, as appropriate:

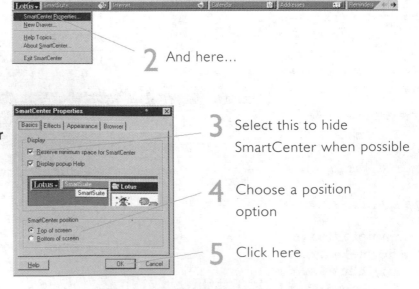

Click here

2 And here...

3 Select this to hide SmartCenter when possible

4 Choose a position option

5 Click here

Re step 3 – if this option is selected, move the mouse pointer to the top or bottom of the screen (as appropriate – see step 4) and click once to make SmartCenter visible.

To hide SmartCenter again, click anywhere outside it.

Working with SmartCenter

HANDY TIP

For ease of use, you can have drawers expand to take up much more of the screen (the precise effect depends on the drawer selected).

Click this button in the top right-hand corner of an active drawer:

To restore the drawer to its original size, click this button:

REMEMBER

You can have more than one drawer open at once.

(For how to use drawers, see the subsequent pages).

Activating drawers

To activate a SmartCenter drawer, move the mouse pointer over it – see the illustration below.

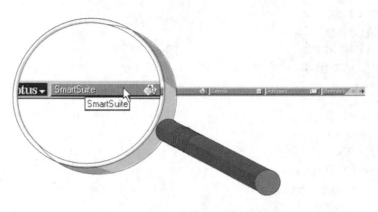

Then click once.

The next illustration shows the Calendar drawer activated.

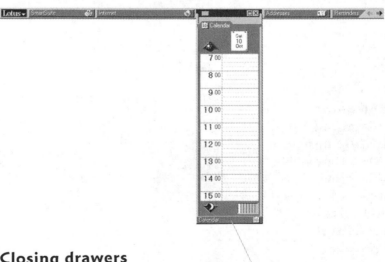

Closing drawers

To close a drawer, click once on the base.

The SmartSuite drawer

You can use the SmartSuite drawer in SmartCenter to:

- launch any SmartSuite Module;

- initiate the creation of a new document based on a SmartMaster, and;

- launch documents you've previously created in the host SmartSuite application.

You can also add shortcuts for non-SmartSuite programs. Simply drag the shortcut icon from your Windows Desktop or Explorer window into empty space in any SmartCenter drawer. Complete any menu/message which appears.

First, launch the SmartSuite drawer using the technique discussed on page 25. Carry out step 1 below. Then do one of the following:

Step 1   to launch a module;

Step 2   to create a new document based on a SmartMaster, or;

Step 3   to launch a previously created file in the relevant SmartSuite module.

Even if you're using Windows 98 and have implemented the Web style desktop, you'll still have to double-click (instead of single-click) on icons in SmartCenter drawers.

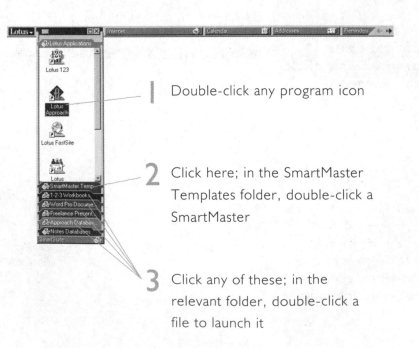

1   Double-click any program icon

2   Click here; in the SmartMaster Templates folder, double-click a SmartMaster

3   Click any of these; in the relevant folder, double-click a file to launch it

The Internet drawer

Drawers which access the Internet use SmartCenter's native browser when there is too much data to display in situ. You can, though, use your own (eg, Internet Explorer). Click this button:

Lotus ▾

In the shortcut menu, click SmartCenter Properties. In the SmartCenter Properties dialog, click the Browser tab. Click System default browser. Finally, click OK.

You can use the Internet drawer in SmartCenter to:

• access various Internet sites, and;

• access Web sites you've saved as Favorites in your Web browser (this feature is a shortcut to your Windows Favorites folder).

Accessing news sites

First, ensure your Internet connection is live. Launch the Internet drawer using the technique discussed on page 25. Then do the following:

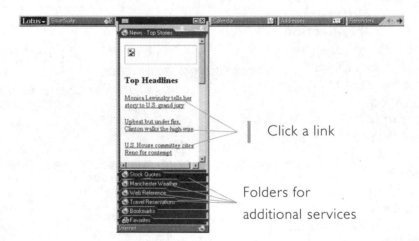

Click a link

Folders for additional services

Additional services you can access via the Internet drawer include:

• Stock quotes;

• Weather;

• Web Reference, and;

• Travel Reservations.

Simply click the relevant folders (see the illustration).

SmartCenter now displays the Web site associated with the link selected in step 1 in:

• its own Web browser, or;

• your default Web browser.

(See the HANDY TIP for how to specify which is used.)

...cont'd

This is the Web browser native to SmartCenter.

If you want to use your own browser, see the HANDY TIP on page 27.

If you have a full-time Internet connection, you can ensure the contents of the Internet folders are updated automatically.

Click a folder tab. In the Folder Properties dialog, click 'Refresh every' and enter the relevant number of minutes. Click OK.

Accessing Favorites

First, ensure your Internet connection is live. Launch the Internet drawer using the technique discussed on page 25. Then do the following:

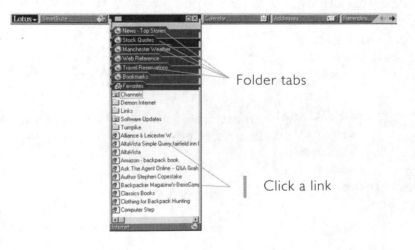

Folder tabs

Click a link

If you don't have a full-time Internet connection, perform a manual update by right-clicking a folder tab and selecting Refresh in the pop-up menu.

The Calendar drawer

To display more than one day, do the following in the Days to Display box:

You can use the Calendar drawer in SmartCenter to:

- enter and view appointments, and;

- have SmartCenter remind you when an appointment is due.

Click a column (eg, to show 4 days, click the 4th column)

Entering appointments

Launch the Calendar drawer using the technique discussed on page 25. Then do the following:

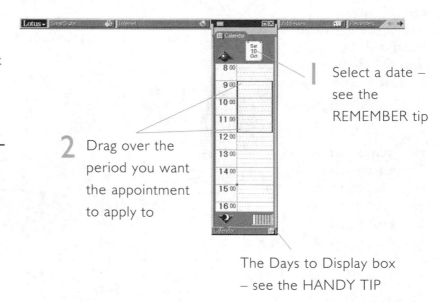

Select a date – see the REMEMBER tip

2 Drag over the period you want the appointment to apply to

Re step 1 – to go to another date, do the following:

Click here

The Days to Display box – see the HANDY TIP

SmartCenter now displays a special dialog; complete steps 3–4 on page 30.

Now click the left or right arrows in this dialog:

to go back or forward by one month respectively. Finally, click the required day.

...cont'd

REMEMBER

You can link the Calendar drawer to your Organizer file (see pages 180–181 for the result).

Right-click the Calendar folder tab. In the pop-up menu, click Folder Properties. In the Folder Properties dialog, click the Calendar tab. In the 'File Type:' field, select Lotus Organizer file. In the 'Name of Lotus Organizer file:' box, type in the name/ address of your Organizer file. Finally, click OK.

HANDY TIP

If you want to be reminded when an appointment is due, launch the Folder Properties dialog (see the REMEMBER tip above). **Click Open drawer, and type in an interval in minutes. Click OK.**

3 Type in appointment details (press Ctrl+Enter to start a new line)

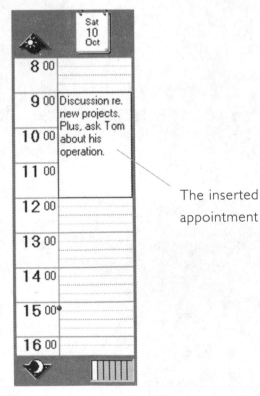

Create Appointment

Description:

Discussion re. new projects.

Plus, ask Tom about his operation.

OK

Cancel

4 Click here

The inserted appointment

The Addresses drawer

You can use the Addresses drawer in SmartCenter to:

* enter and view address details, and;

* view maps for specified areas.

Entering addresses

Launch the Addresses drawer using the technique discussed on page 25. Click the Addresses folder. Then carry out the following steps:

To view address details, click the appropriate letter tab to the left of the folder (eg, to view details for Smith, click S). Now click the entry name. This is the result:

To close the details window, click the cross in the top right corner.

Click the Home tab to enter personal – as opposed to business – information.

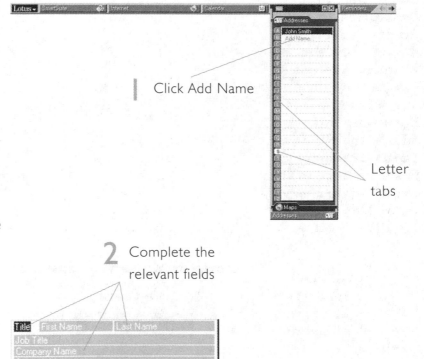

Click Add Name

Letter tabs

2 Complete the relevant fields

3 Click here

You can link the Addresses drawer to your Organizer file (see page 184 for the result).

Right-click the Addresses folder tab. In the pop-up menu, click Folder Properties. In the Folder Properties dialog, click the Name & Address tab. In the File Type: field, select Lotus Organizer file. In the Name of Lotus Organizer file: box, type in the name/address of your Organizer file. Finally, click OK.

Viewing maps

First, ensure your Internet connection is live. Launch the Addresses drawer using the technique discussed on page 25. Then carry out the following steps:

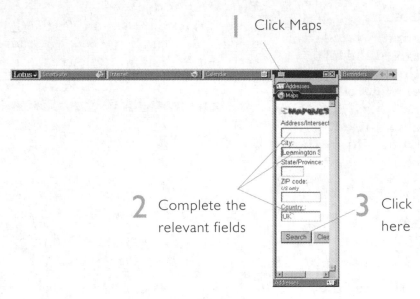

Click Maps

2 Complete the relevant fields

3 Click here

SmartCenter launches its own browser (or your own browser) displaying a map of the selected area:

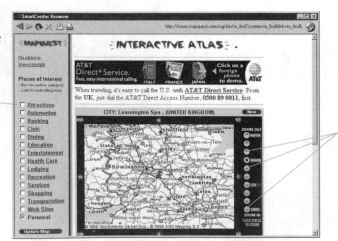

To view features of interest, click one of these: then follow the on-screen instructions.

To zoom in or out, click one of these

To close the browser, press Alt+F4.

Other SmartCenter drawers

The following additional drawers are available:

You can use one further drawer – the Suite Help drawer – in the following ways:

- for help with SmartSuite, click the Help folder. Double-click the SmartSuite Help icon;

- for access to on-line manuals, click the DocOnline folder, then double-click the relevant icon (you must have installed the Acrobat reader for this to work);

- for access to Lotus' on-line sites, ensure your Internet connection is live. Click the Lotus Online folder. Click any link,and;

- for access to on-line tips, ensure your Internet connection is live. Click the SmartSuite Tips folder. Click any tip.

Reminders

To add a reminder, activate the Reminder drawer. Double-click an empty yellow rectangle:

Type in the reminder text and press Enter.

To mark a reminder as completed, click the box to the left (a tick is inserted).

Reference

To look up the definition of a word, click the Dictionary tab. Type in the word and press Enter.

To find synonyms, click the Thesaurus tab. Type in a word and press Enter.

Business Productivity

To access and launch a SmartMaster or template (organised by task rather than application), do the following:

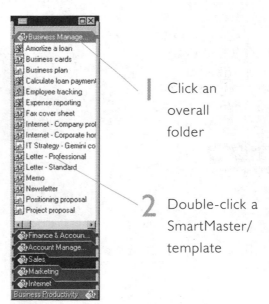

1 Click an overall folder

2 Double-click a SmartMaster/ template

FastSite New in SmartSuite Millennium

FastSite lets you create World Wide Web sites by:

1. assembling a collection of existing document files;

2. converting the existing documents into Web pages, and then;

3. sending these to a server.

The FastSite window – see below – is divided into:

The Site pane   the Web site you build is shown here as a hierarchy

The Tabbed pane   the FastSite window section from which you initiate actions, and in which you can opt to preview your site

Users of SmartSuite 97 must use a different procedure to publish their files to the Web.
  In Word Pro, Approach, 1-2-3 or Freelance Graphics, pull down the File menu and click Internet, Publish as Web Page(s). Click OK. Complete the dialogs which launch.

Title bar   Menu bar

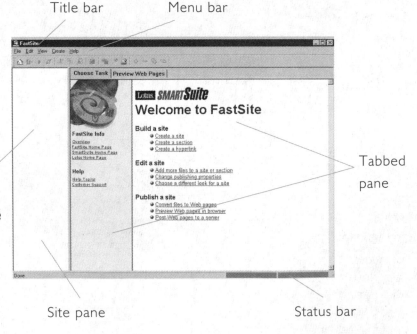

Choose Task | Preview Web Pages

Lotus. SMART Suite
Welcome to FastSite

Build a site
* Create a site
* Create a section
* Create a hyperlink

FastSite Info
Overview
FastSite Home Page
SmartSuite Home Page
Lotus Home Page

Help
Help Topics
Customer Support

Edit a site
* Add more files to a site or section
* Change publishing properties
* Choose a different look for a site

Publish a site
* Convert files to Web pages
* Preview Web pages in browser
* Post Web pages to a server

Tabbed pane

Details of the Web site you create are shown here as a tree – eg:

Site pane   Status bar

Creating a Web site

Creating a Web site is a multi-stage process, which involves:

1. naming the site, applying an Internet-based SmartMaster and creating a home page (table of contents);

2. adding new files as separate pages;

3. converting all the files to Web pages, and;

4. posting all the files to a server.

Stage 1

Start FastSite – see the HANDY TIP – and carry out the following steps:

To start FastSite, click the Windows Start button. Choose Programs, Lotus SmartSuite, Lotus FastSite.

Use FastSite to convert multiple files into HTML format.
   To convert *single* files, on the other hand, use the procedures on pages 22–23.

Ensure this tab is active

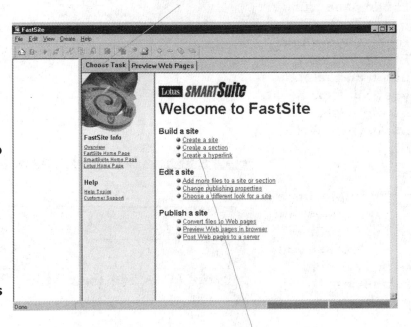

2 Click here

To add a hyperlink to a FastSite page or another Web site, click a home page or section in your site hierarchy. In the Tabbed pane, click Choose Task. Click Create a hyperlink. Click the Action button and select a hyperlink type. Complete the dialog, then click OK.

3 Name your site

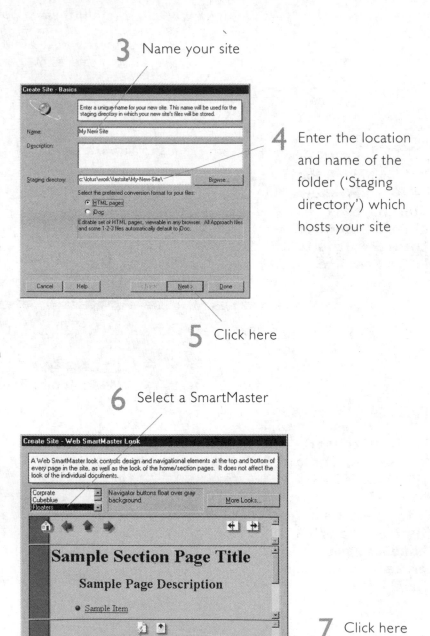

4 Enter the location and name of the folder ('Staging directory') which hosts your site

5 Click here

6 Select a SmartMaster

Clicking a hyperlink on-line takes you to the specified destination straightaway.

7 Click here

...cont'd

FastSite now creates your Web site:

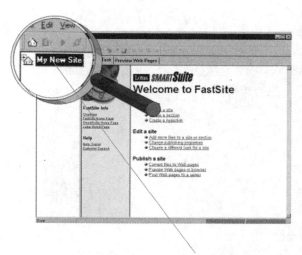

 You can add sections to your Web site. Sections are mini home pages which can themselves hold links to other pages, – use sections to avoid cluttering your hierarchy.

In the Site pane, click the home page under which you want to create a section. In the Tabbed pane, select the Choose Task tab. Click Create a section. FastSite adds a section to your hierarchy:

The new site – the start of a hierarchy in the Site pane

Stage 2

To add pages to your site, carry out the following steps:

If you've created more than one Web site, click the relevant one

Type in a name and press Enter.

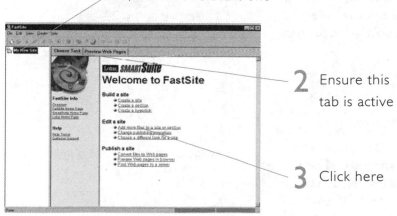

2 Ensure this tab is active

3 Click here

...cont'd

**Re step 5 –
to select
more than
one file,
hold down Ctrl as
you click them.**

**To edit
files
directly
from
within FastSite,
right-click a file in
the hierarchy. Click
Edit Document in
the shortcut menu.
The SmartSuite
module in which the
document was
created launches
with the file already
opened. Make any
editing changes,
then save them in
the normal way.
Close the module.**

**FastSite
tracks
changes
you make
and (for instance)
warns you if you try
to post files to a
server without
updating them.**

4 Click here. In the drop-down list, click the drive/folder combination which hosts the file(s) to be added

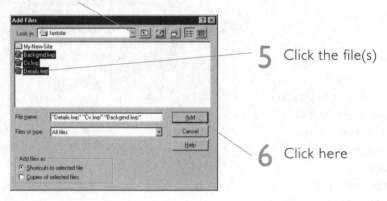

5 Click the file(s)

6 Click here

FastSite adds the new documents to the Site pane hierarchy:

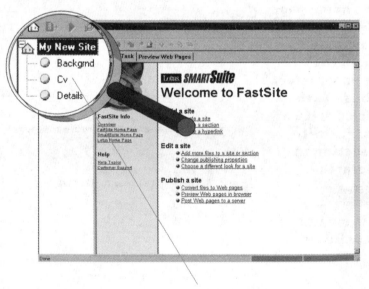

The new documents

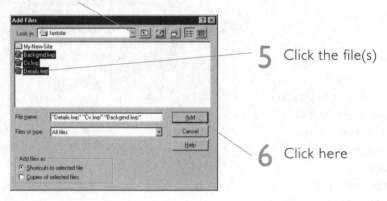

...cont'd

The site hierarchy in the Site pane works like Windows Explorer. You can:

- use drag-and-drop to rearrange the page/ section order;

- delete a page/section by clicking it, pressing Delete and clicking Remove in the resulting message;

- rename a page/ section by right-clicking it, clicking Rename, typing in a new name and pressing Enter, and;

- drag-and-drop files directly from within other windows (eg, Windows Explorer) onto a page or section icon in the hierarchy (this means you can add files without using menus).

Re step 4 – to select more than one entry, hold down Ctrl as you click them.

Stage 3

To convert your files into a Web-based format, do the following:

| If you've created more than one Web site, click the relevant one

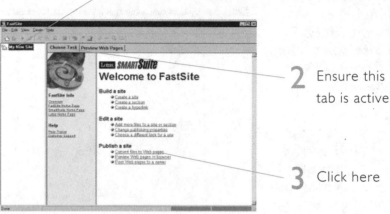

2 Ensure this tab is active

3 Click here

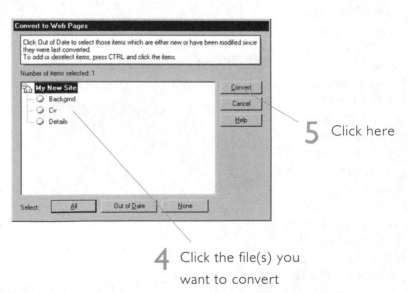

5 Click here

4 Click the file(s) you want to convert

The conversion process now begins – depending on the size of the files involved, it may take some time.

...cont'd

HANDY TIP

You can preview your converted files in FastSite before you complete stage 4. Select the relevant file(s) in the Site pane. Click the Preview Web Pages tab.

REMEMBER

Re step 5 – if you're posting to a network server, FastSite launches a standard Browse dialog; simply choose a drive/folder and click OK. If you're posting to an Internet server, a different dialog appears. Select a server in the FTP servers box (for help with setting up a FTP server, contact your service provider). The dialog expands; select a destination folder then click OK.

Stage 4
To publish your Web site files on a server, do the following:

1 If you've created more than one Web site, click the relevant one

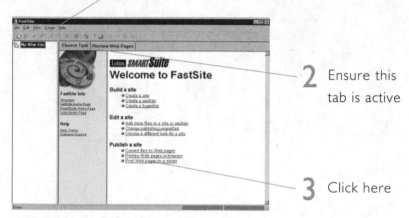

2 Ensure this tab is active

3 Click here

4 Select a server type

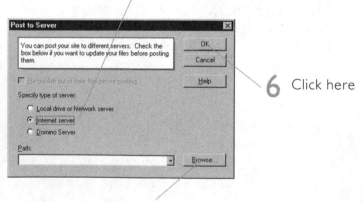

6 Click here

5 Click here to select a server (for how to complete the resulting dialog, see the REMEMBER tip)

Word Pro

Chapter Two

This chapter gives you the basics of using Word Pro. You'll learn how to enter text and negotiate the Word Pro screen. You'll also discover how to format text and create/apply text styles. Finally, you'll learn to insert and work with pictures, dictate text into Word Pro with ViaVoice, and then customise page layout/printing.

Covers

The Word Pro screen

 REMEMBER

The Status bar displays information relating to the active document (eg, what page you're on, the current typeface/ type size and the date/time).

 REMEMBER

This screen is slightly different if ViaVoice is not installed.

 REMEMBER

The ✔ in the menu signifies that the item is currently visible.

 HANDY TIP

Re step 2 – click Clean Screen to hide all extraneous screen components (this increases working space). To return to normal editing, click 🖼 **in the bottom right-hand corner of the screen.**

Below is an illustration of the Word Pro screen.

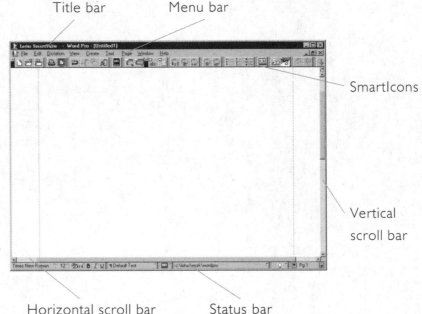

Title bar   Menu bar

SmartIcons

Vertical scroll bar

Horizontal scroll bar   Status bar

Some of these – eg, the scroll bars – are standard to just about all programs which run under Windows. A few of them can be hidden, if required.

Specifying which screen components display

Pull down the View menu. Then do the following:

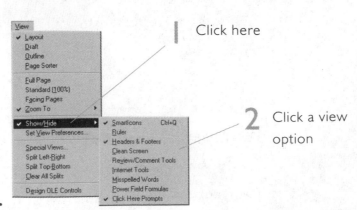

Click here

2 Click a view option

Entering text

Word Pro lets you enter text as soon as you're presented with the basic editing screen. You enter text at the insertion point:

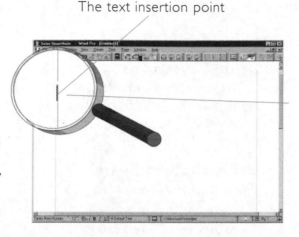

The text insertion point

Begin entering text here

Word Pro has automatic word wrap. This means that you don't have to press Return to enter text on a new line; a new line is automatically started for you, when required. Only press Return if you need to begin a new paragraph.

The procedure for inserting special characters is different in SmartSuite 97. In the File menu, click Text, Insert Other. Complete the dialog which launches. Then click Done.

Special characters

Most of the text you need to enter can be typed in directly from the keyboard. However, it's sometimes necessary to enter special characters (eg, bullets like ☞, or ©). Word Pro lets you do this directly.

Place the insertion point at the correct location. Pull down the Text menu and click Insert Other, Symbol. Do the following:

1 Click here; select a font from the list

2 Double-click a character

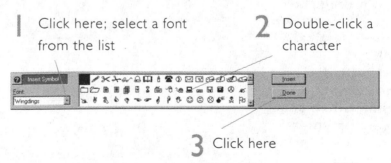

3 Click here

Moving around in documents

The following useful keystroke combinations are unique to Word Pro.

- to move from an Infobox to the open document (and vice versa), hit Alt+Enter
- to go to the start of the next sentence, hit Ctrl+.
- to go to the start of the previous or current sentence, hit Ctrl+,
- to go to the start of the next paragraph, hit Ctrl+↑
- to go to the start of the current paragraph, hit Ctrl+↓

 When you drag the box on the Vertical Scroll bar, SmartSuite displays an indicator showing which page and section you're up to:

You can use the following to move through Word Pro documents:

- keystrokes;
- the vertical/horizontal scroll bars, and;
- the Go To dialog.

Using keystrokes

SmartSuite implements the standard Windows direction keys. Use the left, right, up and down cursor keys in the usual way. Additionally, Home, End, Page Up and Page Down work normally.

Using the scroll bars

Use your mouse to perform any of the following actions:

Click anywhere here to jump to the left or right

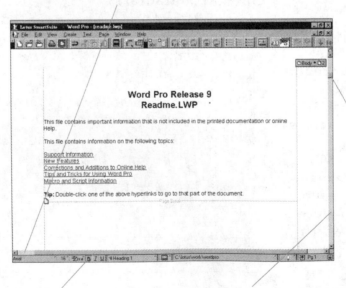

Drag this up or down to move through the active document

Drag this to the left or right to extend the viewing area

Click anywhere here to jump to another location in the document

...cont'd

Using the Go To dialog

You can use the Go To dialog to navigate through the open document.

Pull down the Edit menu and click Go To. Now do the following:

REMEMBER **You can use a keyboard shortcut to launch the Go To dialog: simply press Ctrl+G.**

1 Click here; select a document component from the list

4 Click here

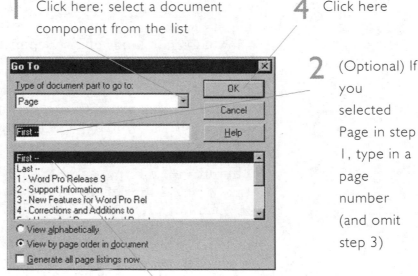

2 (Optional) If you selected Page in step 1, type in a page number (and omit step 3)

3 Click First or Last, to determine direction of movement

REMEMBER **Re step 2 – you can use an alternative technique to move to a specific page. Click any character-based page definition (see 'Refinements...' for more information). Then carry out step 4 after omitting step 3.**

Refinements...

SmartSuite automatically creates definitions of each page within a document by noting the first few characters. As a result, if you select Page in step 1 above, you can opt to move to a specific page *based on recognition of the contents* – see the REMEMBER Tip in the margin for how to do this.

By default, SmartSuite arranges these potted page descriptions in page order. If you want them organised in alphabetical order instead, click View Alphabetically in the dialog above.

Document views – an overview

Word Pro lets you examine your work in various ways, according to the approach you need. It calls these 'views'.

There are three principal views:

Draft

Draft View is used for basic text editing. In Draft View, most formatting elements are still visible: for instance, coloured, emboldened or italicised text displays faithfully. On the other hand, page breaks and headers/footers aren't shown. Certain kinds of inserted pictures display faithfully, others don't.

For these reasons, Draft View is quick and easy to use. It's suitable for bulk text entry and editing. It may not be suitable for use with graphics (for this, switch to Layout view – see below).

Layout

Layout view – the default – works like Draft view, with one exception: it's fully WYSIWYG (What You See Is What You Get), and the positioning of all items on the page is reproduced accurately. What you see is an accurate representation of what your document will look like when printed. Headers and footers are visible, and can be edited directly; margins display faithfully; and all pictures occupy their correct position on-screen.

In Layout view, the screen is updated more slowly. As a result, use it when your document is nearing completion, for final proofing. This suggestion is particularly apt if you're working with a slow computer.

Page Sorter

Page Sorter view is another SmartSuite feature 'borrowed' from high-end Desktop Publishing programs. In Page Sorter view, documents are shown as 'thumbnails' representing individual pages (based on sections and page breaks).

Using views

REMEMBER The view that is currently active has a ✔ against it.

Switching between views
Pull down the View menu. Click Draft, Layout or Page Sorter, as appropriate.

Using Page Sorter
In Page Sorter, you can:

- visually move pages or groups of pages, and;

- expand or contract groups of pages.

When you've launched Page Sorter, carry out step 1 below to move a page or page group. Or follow step 2 to expand or contract a group.

HANDY TIP You can edit text in the normal way within Page Sorter view.

Click a page's title bar; drag it to a new location (the cursor becomes a page icon). Release the mouse button to confirm the move.

HANDY TIP Re step 2 – the lens shows a magnified view of the expand/contract control button. If - (rather than +) displays, clicking it contracts the group.

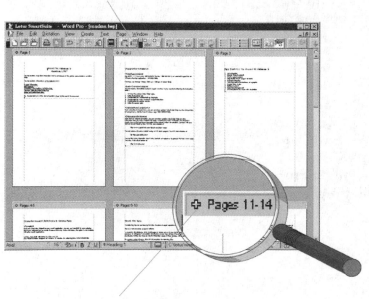

2 Click here to expand a page group

Changing zoom levels

The ability to vary the level of magnification for the active Word Pro document is often useful. Sometimes, it's helpful to 'zoom out' (ie, decrease the magnification) so that you can take an overview; at other times, you'll need to 'zoom in' (increase the magnification) to work in greater detail. Word Pro lets you do either of these very easily.

You can do any of the following:

- choose from preset zoom levels (eg, 100%, 75%);

- specify your own zoom percentage, or;

- choose a zoom setting excluding document margins.

Setting the zoom level

Pull down the View menu. Carry out step 1 below. Then, to apply a preset zoom percentage, follow step 2. Or follow steps 3–5 inclusive to customise the zoom level.

Re step 2 – to exclude margins from the view, select Margin Width.

Click Full Page (Zoom to Full Page, in SmartSuite 97) to have an entire page display.

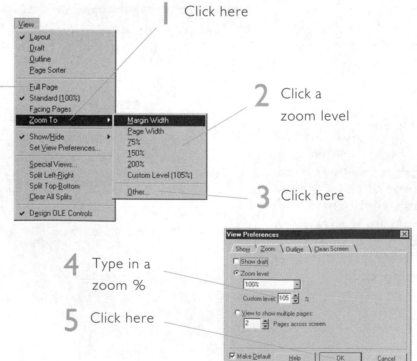

Click here

2 Click a zoom level

3 Click here

4 Type in a zoom %

5 Click here

Formatting text – an overview

Word Pro lets you format text in a variety of ways. Very broadly, however, and for the sake of convenience, text formatting can be divided into two overall categories:

Character formatting

Character formatting is concerned with altering the *appearance* of selected characters. Examples include:

- changing the font;

- changing the type size;

- colouring text;

- changing the font attributes (bold, italic, underlining etc.), and;

- superscripting and subscripting text.

Character formatting is a misnomer in one sense: it can also be applied to specified paragraphs of text, or to parts of specified paragraphs.

Paragraph formatting

Paragraph formatting has to do with the structuring and layout (as well as the appearance) of one or more paragraphs of text.

Examples include:

- specifying paragraph indents/tabs;

- specifying paragraph alignment (eg, left or right justification);

- specifying paragraph and line spacing;

- imposing borders and/or fills on paragraphs;

- applying typefaces and type sizes, and;

- colouring text.

REMEMBER

The distinction between character and paragraph formatting is sometimes blurred: for instance, both can relate to font appearance. When it comes to text styles, however, there is less confusion (see later topics for how to use styles).

Changing the font and/or type size

Character formatting can be changed in two principal ways:

- from within the Text Properties Infobox, and;

- (to a lesser extent) by using 'cycling'.

Using the Text Properties Infobox

First, select the text whose typeface and/or type size you want to amend. Pull down the Text menu and click Text Properties. Now carry out these steps, as appropriate:

SmartSuite uses standard Windows procedures for text selection. However, note the following Word Pro-specific techniques:

- to select a whole sentence, hold down Ctrl and click in it, and;

- to select a whole paragraph, hold down Ctrl and double-click in it.

Click this tab

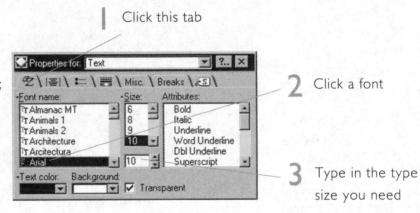

2 Click a font

3 Type in the type size you need

Re step 2 – as well as whole point sizes, you can also enter fractions (to 3 decimal places). For instance, Word Pro will accept 10, 10.6 or 10.879... This level of precision – rare in a word processor – is another feature borrowed from DTP packages.

The changes you make are automatically applied to the selected text.

Using cycling

Select the relevant text and do either of the following:

Click here repeatedly to step up alphabetically through the fonts on your system, one by one

Click here repeatedly to step up through type sizes in increments of 2 (eg, from 6 to 8 to 10...)

Changing text colour

You can change the colour of text:

- from within the Text Properties Infobox, or;

- by using the Status bar.

Using the Infobox

First, select the text you want to alter. Pull down the Text menu and click Text Properties. Now do the following:

Click this tab

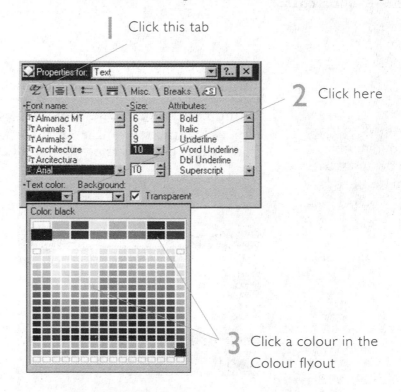

2 Click here

3 Click a colour in the Colour flyout

Using the Status bar

Select the relevant text. Carry out the action indicated below to launch the Colour flyout. Then follow step 3 above.

Click here

Changing font attributes

In Word Pro, the principal typeface attributes you can apply are:

- Bold (**bold**) and Italic (*italic*);

- Underline (<u>underline</u>) and Word Underline (<u>word underline</u>);

- Strikethrough (~~strikethrough~~); Small Caps (SMALL CAPS); Superscript (^{superscript}) and Subscript ($_{subscript}$), and;

- Upper Case (UPPER CASE) and Lower Case (lower case).

You can use the Text Properties Infobox or a specific 'Cycle' SmartIcon to change font attributes.

You can also use keyboard shortcuts:

- Ctrl+B to embolden text;

- Ctrl+I to italicise text;

- Ctrl+U to underline text;

- Ctrl+W to word-underline text (separating spaces are omitted), and;

- Ctrl+N to remove all attributes.

Using the Text Properties Infobox

First, select the relevant text. Pull down the Text menu and click Text Properties. Now do the following:

Click this tab

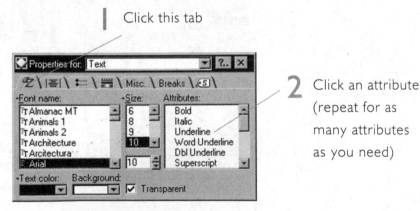

2 Click an attribute (repeat for as many attributes as you need)

Using cycling

First, select the relevant text. Then do the following:

Click here repeatedly to step up through the attributes, one by one

Indenting paragraphs – an overview

You can achieve a similar effect by using tabs. However, indents are easier to apply (and amend subsequently).

Indents are a crucial component of document layout. For instance, in most document types indenting the first line of paragraphs (ie, moving it inwards away from the left page margin) makes the text much more legible.

Other document types – eg, bibliographies – can use the following:

- negative indents (where the direction of indent is towards and beyond the left margin);

- hanging indents (where the first line is unaltered, while subsequent lines are indented), and;

- full indents (where the entire paragraph is indented away from the left and/or right margins).

Don't confuse indents with page margins. Margins are the gap between the edge of the page and the text area; indents define the distance between the margins and text.

Some of the potential indent combinations are shown in the (generic) illustration below:

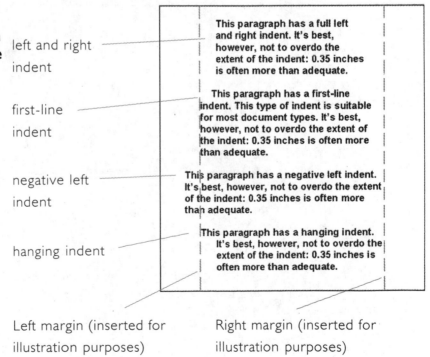

left and right indent

first-line indent

negative left indent

hanging indent

This paragraph has a full left and right indent. It's best, however, not to overdo the extent of the indent: 0.35 inches is often more than adequate.

This paragraph has a first-line indent. This type of indent is suitable for most document types. It's best, however, not to overdo the extent of the indent: 0.35 inches is often more than adequate.

This paragraph has a negative left indent. It's best, however, not to overdo the extent of the indent: 0.35 inches is often more than adequate.

This paragraph has a hanging indent. It's best, however, not to overdo the extent of the indent: 0.35 inches is often more than adequate.

Left margin (inserted for illustration purposes)

Right margin (inserted for illustration purposes)

Indenting paragraphs

Paragraphs can be indented from within the Text Properties Infobox, or by using a 'Cycle' SmartIcon.

Using the Text Properties Infobox

First, select the paragraph you want to indent. Pull down the Text menu and click Text Properties. Now do the following:

The Infobox indent buttons are:

 Left Indent

First Line Indent

 Hanging Indent

Full Indent

Click this tab

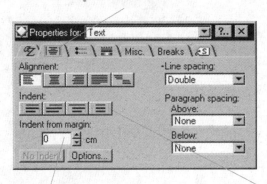

Re step 3 – type in minus values for negative indents.

3 Type in the amount of indent

2 Click an indent button in the indicated row

Using cycling

First, select the relevant text. Then do the following:

Click here repeatedly to step up

through indent types, one by one

Note, however, that the Indent Cycle SmartIcon only applies a Left Indent.

Aligning paragraphs

The following are the principal types of alignment:

Left
Text is flush with the left page margin.

Center
Text is aligned equidistantly between the left and right page margins.

Right
Text is flush with the right page margin.

Justified
Text is flush with the left *and* right page margins

You can align text from within the Text Properties Infobox, or by using a 'Cycle' SmartIcon.

Using the Text Properties Infobox
Select the paragraph(s) you want to indent. Pull down the Text menu and click Text Properties. Now do the following:

The Infobox alignment buttons are:

 Left

Center

Right

Justified

Click this tab

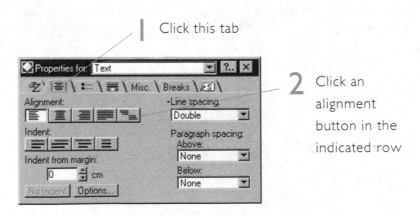

2 Click an alignment button in the indicated row

Using cycling
Select the relevant paragraph(s). Then do the following:

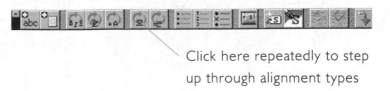

Click here repeatedly to step up through alignment types

Specifying paragraph spacing

As a general rule, set low paragraph spacing settings: a little goes a long way.

72 points are roughly equivalent to one inch (points are used in typography to measure type size).
Picas are an alternative measure (1 pica is almost equivalent to one-sixth of an inch) and are often used to define line length.

Re step 2 – click Multiple to set your own line multiple (and then follow steps 3–4); or click Custom to set your own spacing using a different unit (and then follow steps 5–7).

You can customise the vertical space before and/or after specific text paragraphs. This is a useful device for increasing text legibility.

You can only adjust paragraph spacing from within the Text Properties Infobox.

By default, SmartSuite defines paragraph spacing in terms of preset line measurements (eg, 1½ or 2 lines). However, if none of these are suitable you can specify your own number of lines, or enter measurements in different units (picas, inches, centimetres or points).

Applying paragraph spacing

First, select the paragraph(s) whose spacing you want to adjust. Pull down the Text menu and click Text Properties. Then carry out steps 1–2 below.

Click this tab

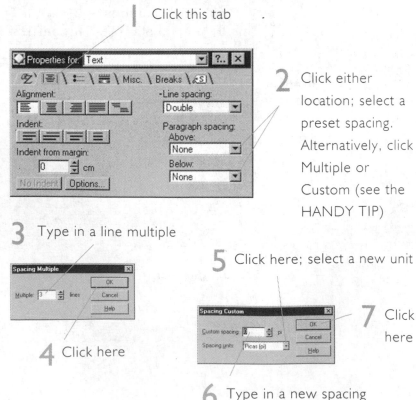

2 Click either location; select a preset spacing. Alternatively, click Multiple or Custom (see the HANDY TIP)

3 Type in a line multiple

4 Click here

5 Click here; select a new unit

6 Type in a new spacing

7 Click here

Line spacing – an overview

It's often necessary to amend line spacing. This is the vertical distance between individual lines of text, or more accurately between the baseline (the imaginary line on which text appears to sit) of one line and the baseline of the previous.

Word Pro lets you apply preset line spacings – Single, ½, 1½ and Double.

Alternatively, you can:

- specify your own line multiples (eg, 4 – four lines);

- specify a number followed by a measurement in inches, centimetres, picas or points (eg, 2 points, 0.167 picas), or;

- specify a leading addition (where the spacing you choose is *added to* the type size). In other words, if you specify a leading adjustment of 4 points on text which is set at 13 points, the resultant spacing is 17 points.

This paragraph is in single line spacing. Newspapers frequently use this.

Single line spacing

This paragraph is in 1½ line spacing. Probably no one uses this, but it serves as a useful illustration.

1½ line spacing

This paragraph is in double line spacing; writers use this when preparing manuscripts

Double line spacing

Adjusting line spacing

First, select the relevant paragraph(s). Then pull down the Text menu and click Text Properties. Carry out steps 1–2, then refer to the REMEMBER tip:

If you've just created a new document, you can set the line spacing before you begin to enter text. Simply leave the insertion point at the start of the document, and then follow the procedures outlined here.

1 Click the Alignment tab

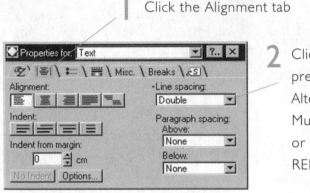

2 Click here; select a preset line spacing. Alternatively, click Multiple, Custom or Leading (see the REMEMBER TIP).

3 Type in a line multiple

Re step 2 – click Multiple to set your own line multiple (and then follow steps 3–4). Or click Custom to set your own spacing using a different unit (and then follow steps 5–7).
   Alternatively, click Leading to set a leading addition (and then follow steps 8–10).

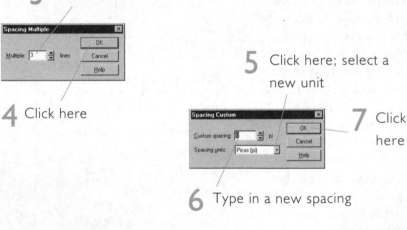

4 Click here

5 Click here; select a new unit

6 Type in a new spacing

7 Click here

8 Click here; select a new unit

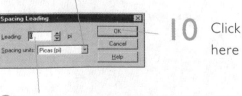

10 Click here

9 Type in a leading addition

Paragraph borders

By default, Word Pro does not border paragraph text. However, you can apply a wide selection of borders if you want. You can specify:

- the border type and thickness;

- how many sides the border should have;

- the border colour;

- whether the bordered text should have a drop shadow, and;

- the distance between the border and the enclosed text.

Applying a border

First, select the paragraph(s) you want to border. Then pull down the Text menu and click Text Properties. Follow steps 1–6, as appropriate (if you carry out step 6, also follow 7).

HANDY TIP

Re step 2 – click the final icon on the right:

if you want to border all four sides of the selected paragraph(s) AND apply a drop shadow.

HANDY TIP

If you want the border to stretch from the left to right margins, click in the Line length field; select To margins.

Click this tab

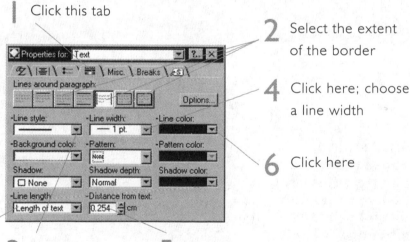

2 Select the extent of the border

4 Click here; choose a line width

6 Click here

3 Click here; choose a line style

5 Type in a separation distance

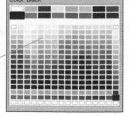

7 Choose a colour

Working with tabs

Tabs are a means of indenting the first line of text paragraphs (you can also use indents for this purpose, although tabs are probably more convenient for single paragraphs).

Never use the Space bar to indent paragraphs: spaces vary in size according to the typeface and type size applied to specific paragraphs.

When you press the Tab key while the text insertion point is at the start of a paragraph, the text in the first line jumps to the next tab stop. This is a useful way to increase the legibility of your text. Word Pro lets you set tab stops with great precision.

By default, tab stops are inserted automatically every quarter of an inch. If you want, however, you can enter new or revised tab stop positions individually.

Setting tab stops

First, select the paragraph(s) in which you need to set tab stops. Pull down the Text menu and click Text Properties. Follow steps 1–3 below:

Click the Misc tab

Re step 2 – if you don't want to enter a series of tabs, choose From left edge (to enter a tab relative to the left margin) or From right edge (to enter one relative to the right margin). Alternatively, click Remove Local Tabs to remove previously assigned tab settings.

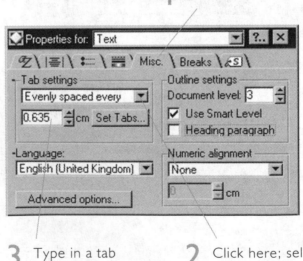

3 Type in a tab setting

2 Click here; select a tab distribution in the drop-down list

Searching for text

Word Pro lets you search for specific text within the active document.

You can also search for special characters. For example, you can look for paragraph marks, tabs, carets (^) and wildcards.

You can also:

When you've finished using the Find & Replace bar, click this button:

Done

- limit the search to words which match the case of the text you specify (eg, if you search for 'Arm', SmartSuite will not flag 'arm' or 'ARM'), or;

- limit the search to whole words (eg, if you search for 'eat', SmartSuite will not flag 'beat' or 'seat').

Re step 3 – click the left-pointing arrow to search backwards, or the right-pointing arrow to search towards the end of the document.

Initiating a text search

Pull down the Edit menu and click Find & Replace Text. Now carry out the following steps, as appropriate:

1   Type in the text you want to find   3   Click a search direction

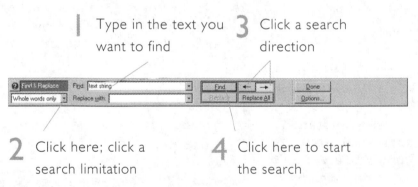

2   Click here; click a search limitation   4   Click here to start the search

The SmartSuite wildcards – '^?' and '^*' – are especially useful.
  For instance, searching for 'me^?t' would find 'meet' or 'meat'. Searching for 'le^*' would find 'lend', 'leap', 'lexicography' etc.

Entering codes

When you complete step 1, you can enter the following:

^ t	Tab
^ r	Paragraph mark
^ ^	^
^ ?	any one character
^ *	any number of characters (to the end of the word)
^ +	any number of characters (across multiple words)

Replacing text

When you've searched for and located text in the active document, you can have Word Pro replace it automatically with the text of your choice.

You can customise find-and-replace operations with the same parameters as a simple find operation. For example, you can make them case-specific, or only replace whole words. You can also incorporate a variety of codes (for how to do this, see the 'Searching for text' topic earlier in this section). For instance, you could have Word Pro locate instances of two paragraph marks and replace them with a single mark...

There is, however, one way in which find-and-replace operations differ from find operations: wildcards can't be incorporated in replacement text.

When you've finished using the Find & Replace bar, click this button:

Initiating a find-and-replace operation

First pull down the Edit menu and click Find & Replace Text. Now follow steps 1 and 2 below. Carry out steps 3 and 4, as appropriate. Finally, follow step 5 to perform all valid find-and-replace operations automatically (or see the REMEMBER tip):

REMEMBER If you don't want all instances of the text replaced immediately, don't carry out step 5. Instead, click the Find button after step 4. When the first match has been found, click Replace. Repeat this as often as necessary.

1 Type in the text you want to find

2 Type in the replacement text

3 Click a search direction

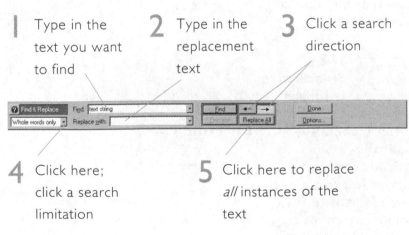

4 Click here; click a search limitation

5 Click here to replace *all* instances of the text

Working with headers

You can have Word Pro display and print text at the top of each page within a document; the area of the page where repeated text appears is called the 'header'. In the same way, you can have text printed at the base of each page; in this case, the relevant page area is called the 'footer'. Headers and footers are printed within the top and bottom page margins, respectively.

Headers and footers are commonly used to display document titles, origination details and page numbers.

Inserting a header

In Layout view (headers and footers are not visible in Draft view), move to the top of the first page, then click in the Header area. Now do the following:

Type in the Header text

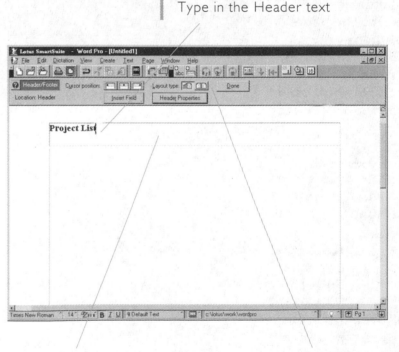

The Header area   Header/Footer bar   New in SmartSuite Millennium

Working with footers

To edit an existing footer, simply follow the procedure outlined here; in step 1, amend the current footer text.

You can have Word Pro automatically display and print text at the bottom of each page within a document. The area of the page where this repeated text appears is called the 'footer'.

Footers are often used to display an abbreviated version of the document's title and/or the page number.

Inserting a footer

In Layout view, move to the bottom of the first page then click in the Footer area. Do the following:

Re step 1 – to have Word Pro insert a special code which automatically inserts the page number in the footer, Millennium edition users can click this button in the Header/Footer bar:

In the drop-down list, click Page Number.

Type in the Footer text

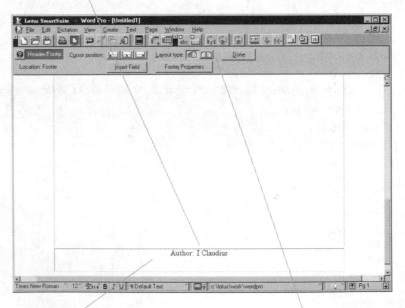

The Footer area   Header/Footer bar   New in SmartSuite Millennium

Re step 1 – users of SmartSuite 97 should follow a different procedure to insert page numbers.
Click Insert Page Number in the Text menu. Click OK.

Undo

To set the number of Undo levels, pull down the File menu and click User Setup, Word Pro Preferences. In the Word Pro Preferences dialog, click the General tab. In the Undo levels field, type in the number. Click OK.

Don't set too many Undo levels – this can slow down your computer unacceptably (because Word Pro has to store details of editing actions in memory).

The precise text of the menu entry above depends on the action being undone.

Word Pro lets you reverse – 'undo' – most editing operations.

You can undo the last editing action in the following ways:

- via the keyboard;

- from within the Edit menu, or;

- by using a SmartIcon.

Using the keyboard
Simply press Ctrl+Z to undo an action.

Using the Edit menu
Pull down the Edit menu. To undo an action, do the following:

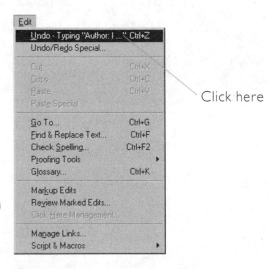

Click here

Using the Undo SmartIcon
To undo an operation, click the following SmartIcon in the overhead SmartIcon bar:

Text styles – an overview

HANDY TIP

Word Pro has a feature called SmartCorrect which corrects errors automatically. For instance, if you often type 'ocur' for 'occur' or 'teh' for 'the', Word Pro will correct these as soon as you press the Spacebar after the word.

To ensure SmartCorrect is enabled (the default), pull down the File menu and click User Setup, Word Pro Preferences. Click the Enable tab in the Word Pro Preferences dialog. In the General usage section, ensure SmartCorrect is ticked. Click OK.

Styles are named collections of associated formatting commands. Word Pro makes extensive use of styles in all areas, but particularly when it comes to text formatting.

The advantage of using styles is that you can apply more than one formatting enhancement to selected text in one go. Once a style is in place, you can easily change one or more elements of it and have Word Pro apply the amendments automatically throughout the whole of the active document. This results in an enormous saving in time and effort.

New (blank) documents you create in Word Pro contain a variety of pre-defined styles. These include:

Body Single	–	used for text which forms the body of a document
Default Text	–	ditto
Bullet 1 and *Bullet 2*	–	creates bulleted lists
Heading 1	–	used for headings
Heading 2	–	ditto (but smaller)
Heading 3	–	ditto (even smaller)
Title	–	a bold heading
Number List	–	creates automatically numbered lists
First Line Indent	–	automatically applies a preset paragraph indent

Other SmartMasters/templates have many more preset styles. (Some are context-dependent, eg, *Default Page* only applies to page settings, not specific text.)

You can easily create (and apply) your own styles.

Creating a text style

Creating a style is a simple, three-stage process:

A. apply the appropriate formatting enhancements to specific text;

B. click in the text (or select it), and then;

C. tell Word Pro to save this formatting as a style.

First, carry out A–B above. Then pull down the Text menu and click Text Properties. Now do the following:

Click the Style tab

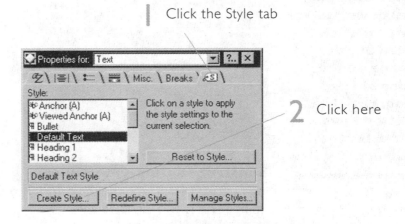

2 Click here

5 Click here

HANDY TIP

If you want to create a character (as opposed to a paragraph) style, click the arrow to the right of the Style type field; select Character in the drop-down list.

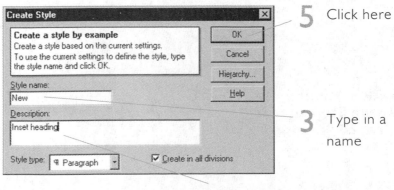

3 Type in a name

4 (Optional) Type in a description

See 'Applying a text style' on the following page for how to use your new style.

Applying a text style

Word Pro makes applying styles easy.

Users of the Millennium edition can assign function keys to styles, so that they can be applied with just a single keystroke.

Pull down the Text menu and click Named Styles, Manage. In the Manage Styles dialog, click the Function Keys button. Do the following:

First, select the text you want to apply the style to. Or, if you only want to apply it to a single paragraph, place the insertion point inside it. Pull down the Text menu and click Text Properties. Now do the following:

Click the Style tab

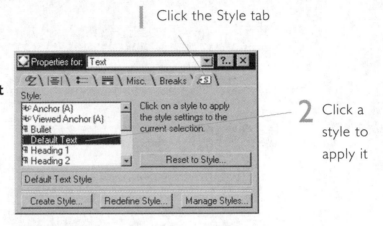

2 Click a style to apply it

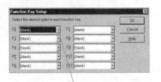

Click a function key box and select a style. Click OK

Back in the Manage Styles dialog, click Close.

Shortcut for applying styles

Word Pro provides a shortcut which makes it even easier to apply styles: you can use the Style button on the Status bar at the base of the screen.

Select the text you want to apply the style to. Then do the following:

2 Click a style

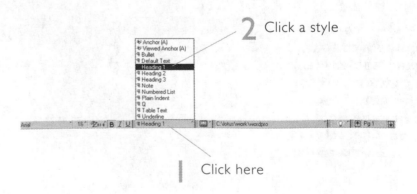

Click here

Amending a text style

When you redefine a style, all other instances of the style in the open document are automatically updated accordingly.

The easiest way to modify an existing style is to:

A. use the Text Properties Infobox to apply the appropriate formatting enhancements to text (see earlier topics for information on how to do this) and then select it, and then;

B. tell Word Pro to redefine the associated style based on your amendments.

First, carry out A. above. Then do the following:

Click the Style tab

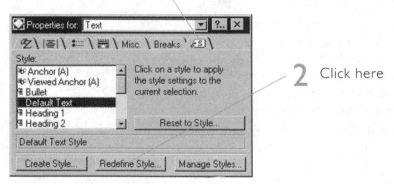

2 Click here

You can copy styles from one document into another.
Pull down the Text menu and click Named Styles, Manage. In the Manage Styles dialog, click Copy From. In the Copy Styles From dialog, click the Browse button. Use the Browse dialog to select a file. Click Open. Back in the Copy Styles From dialog, select one or more styles; click Copy to copy them into the host document.

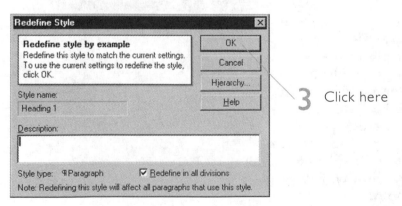

3 Click here

Style management

Good housekeeping sometimes makes it necessary to remove unwanted styles from the active document. Word Pro lets you do this very easily.

Deleting styles

Pull down the Text menu and click Text Properties. Now do the following:

Click the Style tab

HANDY TIP

You can delete more than one style at a time. Simply repeat step 3 as often as required, then follow steps 4–6 as normal.

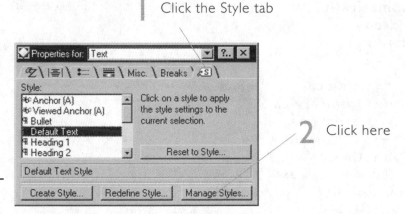

2 Click here

REMEMBER

You can also use this dialog to rename a specified style. Simply follow step 3, then click the Rename button. In the To field in the Rename Style dialog, type in a new name. Then click OK. Finally, follow step 6.

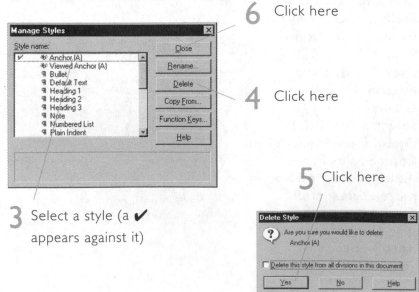

6 Click here

4 Click here

5 Click here

3 Select a style (a ✔ appears against it)

Spell-checking text

Word Pro makes use of two separate dictionaries. One – LTSUSER1.UDC – can be thought of as yours. When you follow step 4, the flagged word is stored in this and recognised in future checking sessions.

Re step 1 – if the flagged word isn't correct and Word Pro's suggestions are also wrong, type in the correct version in the Replace with field. Then carry out step 2 or 3.

Click the Done button when you're ready to close the Spell Check bar.

To check all the text within the active document in one go, pull down the Edit menu and click Check Spelling. Word Pro launches its Spell Check bar, highlights all words it doesn't recognise within the current document and takes you to the first (flagged with a different colour). Usually, it provides alternative suggestions; if one of these is correct, you can opt to have it replace the flagged word. You can do this singly (ie, just this instance is replaced) or globally (where all future instances – within the current checking session – are replaced).

Alternatively, you can have SmartSuite:

• ignore *this* instance of the flagged word and resume checking;

• ignore *all* future instances of the word and resume checking, or;

• add the word to your personal dictionary and resume checking.

Carry out step 1 below (if Word Pro has produced a viable suggestion), then follow step 2 or 3. Alternatively, perform any one of steps 4, 5 and 6.

1 Click a suggestion then follow step 2 OR 3

3 Or click here to replace all future instances

2 Click here to replace this instance

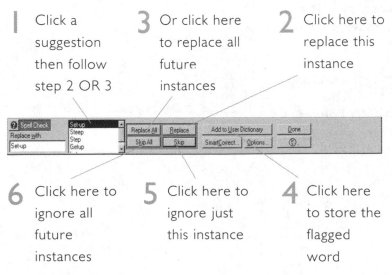

6 Click here to ignore all future instances

5 Click here to ignore just this instance

4 Click here to store the flagged word

Searching for synonyms

Word Pro lets you search for synonyms while you're editing the active document. You do this by calling up the resident Thesaurus. The Thesaurus categorises words into meanings, and each meaning is allocated various synonyms from which you can choose.

The Thesaurus works in two ways. You can flag a word in the document and have it propose synonyms (the more usual method). Alternatively, you can enter words *directly* into the Thesaurus and request suggestions.

Using the Thesaurus

First, select the word for which you require a synonym (or simply position the insertion point within it). Pull down the Edit menu and click Proofing Tools, Check Thesaurus. Now do the following:

Users of SmartSuite 97 should click Check Thesaurus in the Edit menu instead.

To look up a word which isn't in the current document, type it into the Word to look up or to be replaced field. Then click the Lookup button. Now carry out steps 1–3, as appropriate.

To close the Thesaurus dialog, press Alt+F4.

The selected word appears here

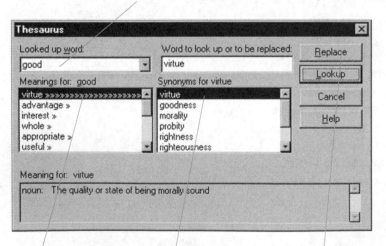

1 Click the appropriate meaning

2 Click the synonym you want to replace the selected word

3 Click here to substitute the synonym for the selected word

Working with pictures – an overview

You can have text flow around pictures – this is called 'text wrap'.
Right-click the picture frame. In the shortcut menu, click Frame Properties. In the Frame Properties Infobox, click the Placement tab. Choose from these wrap options:

 Behind

 Above & below

 Both sides

 On left side

 On right side

 On widest side

Users of the Millennium edition can wrap text around irregularly shaped graphics frames. Click Irregular wrap in the Placement tab of the Frame Properties Infobox.

The Word Pro module lets you add colour or greyscale pictures to the active document. Pictures – also called graphics – include:

- drawings produced in other programs;

- clip art, and;

- scanned photographs.

Use pictures – whatever their source – to add much needed visual impact to documents. But use them judiciously: too much colour can be off-putting, and ultimately self-defeating.

Pictures are stored in various third-party formats. These formats are organised into two basic types:

Bitmap images
Bitmaps consist of pixels (dots) arranged in such a way that they form a graphic image. Because of the very nature of bitmaps, the question of 'resolution' – the sharpness of an image expressed in dpi (dots per inch) – is very important. Bitmaps look best if they're displayed at their native resolution. Word Pro can manipulate a wide variety of third-party bitmap graphics formats. These include PCX, TIF and GIF.

Vector images
You can also insert vector graphics files into Word Pro documents. Vector images (eg, CGM) consist of and are defined by algebraic equations. Less complex than bitmaps, they contain less detail. Vector files can also include bitmap information.

Irrespective of the format type, SmartSuite can incorporate pictures with the help of special 'filters'. These are special mini-programs whose job it is to translate third-party formats into a form which SmartSuite can use.

Brief notes on picture formats

Graphics formats Word Pro will accept include the following (the column on the left shows the relevant file suffix):

BMP   The native Windows bitmap format. Frequently used.

CGM   Computer Graphics Metafile. A vector format frequently used in the past, especially as a medium for clip-art transmission. Less often used nowadays.

CDR   Files produced by version 3 of the popular drawing package CorelDRAW! from Corel Corporation. (Some later versions of CorelDRAW! will happily export files to version 3's format).

EPS   Encapsulated PostScript. Perhaps the most widely used PostScript format. PostScript combines vector *and* bitmap data very successfully. Incorporates a low-resolution bitmap 'header' for preview purposes.

GIF   Graphics Interchange Format. Developed for the on-line transmission of graphics data across the CompuServe network. Just about any Windows program – and a lot more besides – will read GIF. Disadvantage: it can't handle more than 256 colours. Compression is supported.

PCD   (Kodak) PhotoCD. Used primarily to store photographs on CD.

PCX   An old standby. Originated with PC Paintbrush, a paint program. Used for years to transfer graphics data between Windows applications.

TIF   TIFF, or Tagged Image File Format. If anything, even more widely used than PCX, across a whole range of platforms and applications.

Inserting pictures

First, position the insertion point at the location within the active document where you want to insert the picture. Pull down the File menu and do the following:

REMEMBER **Word Pro creates special 'snapshot' files for inserted pictures. These enable it to display pictures rapidly in open documents.**

Click here

3 Click here. In the drop-down list, click the drive/folder that hosts the file

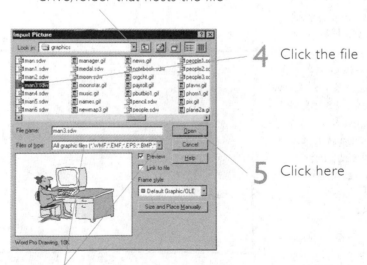

4 Click the file

HANDY TIP **Make sure Preview is selected for an indication of what a picture will look like when inserted.**

5 Click here

2 Make sure the relevant file type is shown. If it isn't, click the arrow and select it from the drop-down list

Manipulating pictures – an overview

Once you've inserted pictures into a Word Pro document, you can amend them in a variety of ways. You can:

- rescale them;

- apply a border;

- move them, or;

- rotate them.

Selecting an image

To carry out any of these operations, you have to select the relevant picture first. To do this, simply position the mouse pointer over the image and left-click once. Word Pro surrounds the image with eight handles (and also with a frame – see the tip on the left). Handles are positioned at the four corners, and midway on each side. The illustration below demonstrates these (two of the handles are magnified for convenience):

 By default, Word Pro surrounds inserted graphics with a frame (although it can be invisible – see page 78 for how to achieve this). Frames make pictures easier to manipulate, and even have their own Frame Properties Infobox.

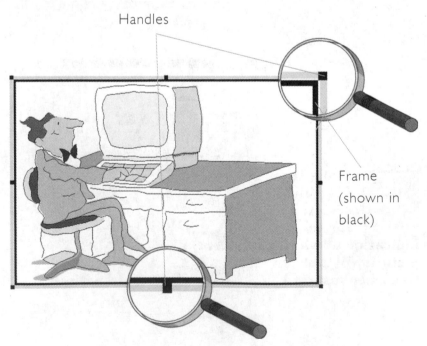

Handles

Frame (shown in black)

Rescaling pictures

There are two ways in which you can rescale pictures:

- proportionately, where the height/width ratio remains constant, or;

- disproportionately, where the height/width ratio is disrupted (this is sometimes called 'warping' or 'skewing').

To rescale a picture, first select it. Then move the mouse pointer over:

- one of the corner handles, if you want to rescale the image in any direction, or;

- one of the handles in the middle of the sides, if you want to rescale it laterally.

In either eventuality, the mouse pointer changes to a double-headed arrow. Click and hold down the left mouse button. Drag outwards to increase the image size or inwards to decrease it. Release the mouse button to confirm the change.

 By default, Word Pro rescales images proportionately. To warp a picture, do the following before you rescale it.

With the image selected, click Frame Properties in the Frame menu. In the Frame Properties Infobox, click this tab:

Now deselect Scale proportionately.

 Re the above tip, users of SmartSuite 97 should activate the Misc tab in the Frame Properties dialog instead.

Another Word Pro image, this time skewed from the right inwards

Bordering pictures

By default, Word Pro applies an even border to inserted pictures (within the holding frame). However, you can change this, if you want. You can specify:

- the border type and thickness;

- whether the bordered image should have a drop shadow;

- how many sides the border should have, and;

- the border colour.

Applying a border

Select the image whose border you want to amend. Pull down the Frame menu and click Frame Properties. Follow steps 1–6, as needed (if you carry out step 6, also follow 7).

HANDY TIP

Re step 2 – click the following icon:

if you want to border all four sides of the picture AND apply a drop shadow.

HANDY TIP

Re step 2 – click the following icon:

none

if you want the picture border to be invisible.

1 Click this tab

2 Select a border icon (to specify the extent)

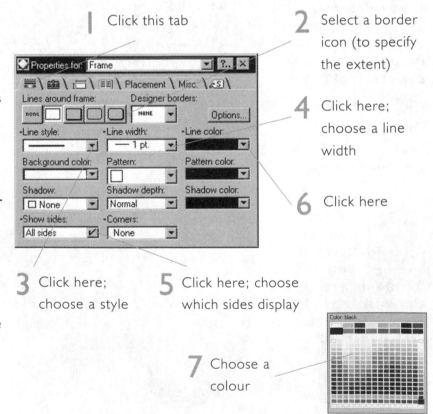

4 Click here; choose a line width

6 Click here

3 Click here; choose a style

5 Click here; choose which sides display

7 Choose a colour

Moving pictures

Millennium edition users can rotate BMP or TIF pictures.

Right-click the picture frame. In the shortcut menu, click Frame Properties. Click this tab:

Click the Rotate Image box (if this is greyed out, see the HANDY TIP below), and select Other. Type in a % and click OK.

HANDY TIP

Only BMP and TIF files can be rotated.
However, Word Pro lets you convert other formats into BMP.

Right-click the picture frame. In the shortcut menu, click # Object, Convert (where # is the picture format). In the Convert dialog, select Bitmap in the Object type field. Click OK.

You can easily move pictures from one location on the page to another.

First, click the image to select it. Move the mouse pointer over it; it changes to an open hand. Left-click once and hold down the button. Drag the picture to its new location.

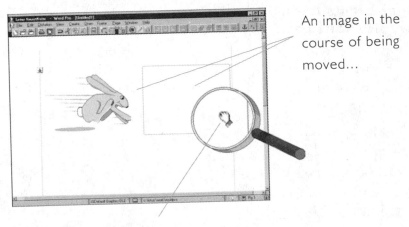

An image in the course of being moved...

The Move cursor

Release the mouse button to confirm the move.

Problems with Move operations?

If you find that dragging pictures has little or no effect, select the image. Pull down the Frame menu and click Frame Properties. Carry out the following steps:

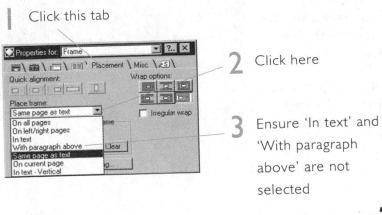

1 Click this tab

2 Click here

3 Ensure 'In text' and 'With paragraph above' are not selected

Preparing to use ViaVoice

REMEMBER

You need the following minimum system requirements to run ViaVoice at its best:

- 150 Mhz Pentium processor with MMX;
- 32 Mb RAM (48 Mb for Windows NT);
- 125 Mb hard disk space;
- a good-quality sound card, and;
- a CD-ROM drive.

HANDY TIP

Re the above tip – ViaVoice will run on systems with a *slightly* slower processor. However, you should ensure that you've carried out the full enrolment process as this optimises performance.

SmartSuite comes with a special edition of IBM ViaVoice which is designed to work with Word Pro. ViaVoice lets you dictate text without typing (but see the REMEMBER tip for system requirements, which are especially stringent).

Before you can use ViaVoice, however, you need to:

1. set up the microphone which accompanies ViaVoice, then;

2. complete an 'enrolment' process. ViaVoice already understands English, but it needs to learn to recognise your individual speech patterns. You achieve this by reading out prepared phrases; this is enrolment.

Microphone setup

Do the following:

2 Click all three locations

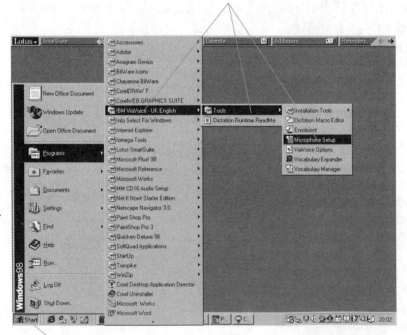

Click here

...cont'd

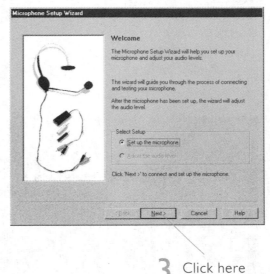

3 Click here

 The choice you make in step 4 determines which dialogs appear after step 6.

4 Select a speaker type

 Complete the further dialogs which launch after step 6. ViaVoice tests your audio setup and helps you adjust your headset and insert the relevant microphone jacks. You'll also repeat specific words so ViaVoice knows your microphone is working correctly.

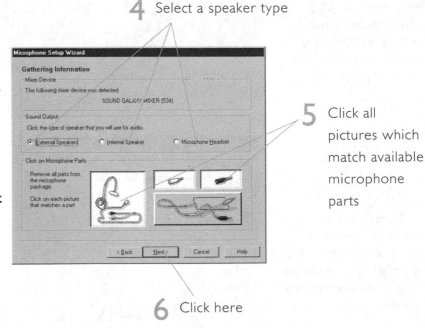

5 Click all pictures which match available microphone parts

6 Click here

...cont'd

 You may have already performed enrolment during installation of ViaVoice.

If so, ignore steps 1–8 on this and the opposite page.

Enrolment
Do the following:

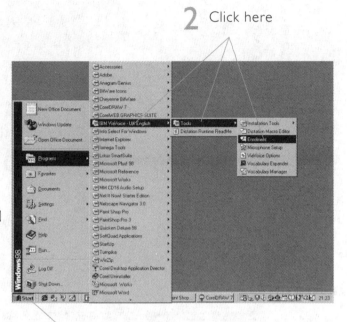

2 Click here

Click here

 You should carry out enrolment in the same conditions which will apply when you dictate text. For example:

• your microphone should be in the same position, and;

• the ambient noise level should be more or less identical.

If your voice changes for any reason (eg, you have a cold), you should perform enrolment again.

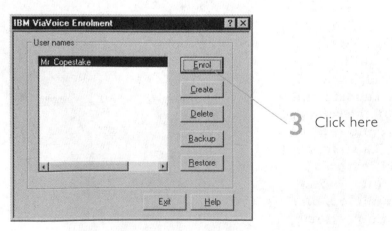

3 Click here

...cont'd

4 Ensure this is selected

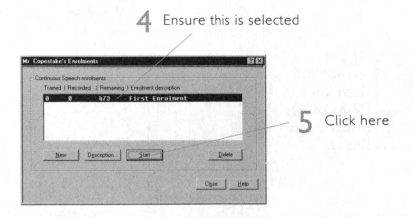

5 Click here

 HANDY TIP

Follow step 6 for a guide to how to speak when using ViaVoice.

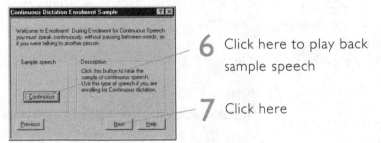

6 Click here to play back sample speech

7 Click here

REMEMBER

After step 8, ViaVoice displays a succession of simple phrases here: repeat each one. ViaVoice analyses it and moves on automatically to the next.

Continue to the end – the entire enrolment process should take well over an hour.

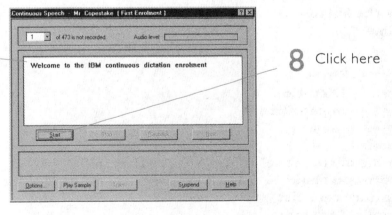

8 Click here

Using ViaVoice

To begin dictating in Word Pro, pull down the Dictation menu and do the following:

 If you haven't installed ViaVoice, the Dictation menu is unavailable.

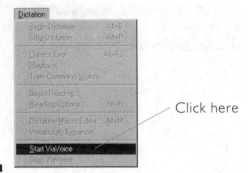

Click here

 Before you start to dictate, ensure the Microphone icon in the ViaVoice bar:

The Word Pro screen now changes (a lengthy process) – the ViaVoice bar displays:

ViaVoice bar

is green. If it isn't, click it.

If you want to turn off the microphone, click the button again.

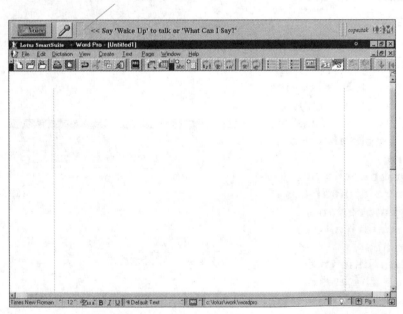

 Re 'Dictation' on page 85 – say:

'What Can I Say?' **into the microphone (before you begin dictating) for a list of available verbal commands.**

ViaVoice provides a spoken welcome.

...cont'd

To have ViaVoice convert text back into speech, select it. Pull down the Dictation menu and click Begin Reading. A small window with an animated face appears:

The window closes when the reading is finished.

When you're dictating in ViaVoice, you can't carry out standard keyboard editing.

To close down ViaVoice when you've finished dictating, pull down the Dictation menu and click Stop ViaVoice.

Dictation

Place the insertion point at the relevant location and say 'Wake Up' into the microphone, followed by 'Begin dictation'. ViaVoice responds by saying 'Begin dictating' and inserts this into the screen:

Begin Dictating...

Dictate the text you want to insert, but bear in mind the following:

1. ViaVoice is a continuous-speech dictation program, so speak in complete phrases with no undue pauses between individual words.

2. Be sure to speak clearly and in a measured way, and don't over-enunciate words.

3. Avoid interrupting sentences, as far as possible, as this makes ViaVoice hesitant.

When you've finished dictating, say 'Stop Dictation' into the microphone.

Correcting errors

Sometimes, ViaVoice will insert the wrong word. To correct it, ensure dictation has been terminated (see above). Right-click the incorrect word. In the shortcut menu, click Correct Error. Do ONE of the following:

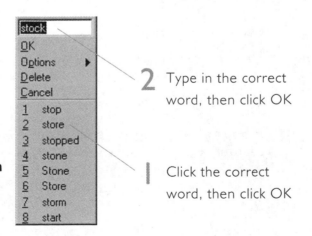

2 Type in the correct word, then click OK

Click the correct word, then click OK

Page setup – an overview

You can control the following aspects of page layout in the Word Pro module:

- the top, bottom, left and/or right page margins;

- the distance above the header (between the top page edge and the top edge of the header), and;

- the distance below the footer (between the bottom page edge and the bottom edge of the footer).

The illustration below shows the principal components:

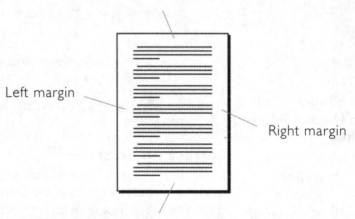

Top margin (including header)

Left margin

Right margin

Bottom margin (including footer)

You can also specify:

- the overall page size (inclusive of margins and headers/ footers), and;

- the page orientation ('landscape' or 'portrait').

If none of the supplied page sizes is suitable, you can even customise your own.

Specifying margins

Margin settings are the framework on which indents and tabs are based.

All documents have margins because they need a certain amount of 'white space' (the unprinted portion of the page) to balance the areas which contain text and graphics. Margins make documents more visually effective.

Customising document margins

Pull down the Page menu and click Page Properties. Now do the following:

Users of SmartSuite 97 should follow a different procedure to launch the Page Layout infobox: pull down the File menu and click Document Properties, Page.

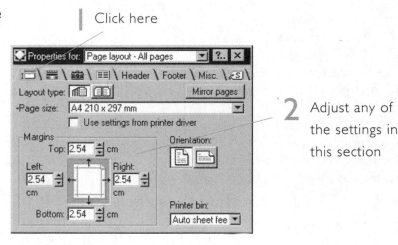

Click here

2 Adjust any of the settings in this section

Customising header/footer margins

To adjust header margins, pull down the Page menu and click Page Properties. Now do the following:

To amend footer margins, launch the Page Layout Infobox, as here. Click the Footer tab. Now adjust the Below footer field.

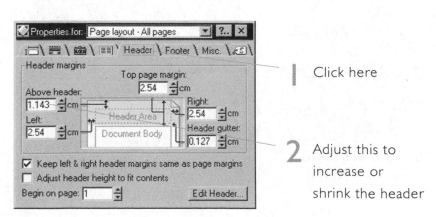

1 Click here

2 Adjust this to increase or shrink the header

Specifying the page size

Word Pro comes with several preset page sizes. These are suitable for most purposes. However, if you need to, you can also set up your own page definition.

There are two aspects to every page size:

- a vertical measurement, and;

- a horizontal measurement.

There are two possible orientations:

Users of SmartSuite 97 should follow a different procedure to launch the Page Layout infobox: pull down the File menu and click Document Properties, Page.

Portrait   Landscape

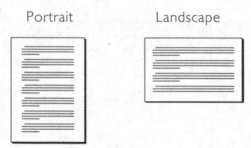

Setting the page size

First, position the insertion point at the location within the active document from which you want the new page size to apply. Then pull down the Page menu and click Page Properties. Perform step 1 below, then 2 and/or 3:

To create your own page size, click Custom in step 2. Then type in height and width measurements (see below):

Click here

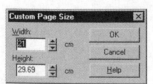

Click OK. Finally, carry out step 3.

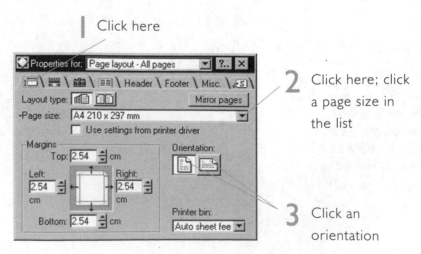

2 Click here; click a page size in the list

3 Click an orientation

Print setup

Most Word Pro documents need to be printed eventually. Before you can begin printing, however, you need to ensure that:

- the correct printer is selected (if you have more than one installed), and;

- the correct printer settings are in force.

SmartSuite calls these collectively 'Print Setup'.

Irrespective of the printer selected, the settings (step 2 below) vary in accordance with the job in hand. For example, most printer drivers (the software that 'drives' the printer) allow you to specify whether or not you want pictures printed. Additionally, they often allow you to specify the resolution or print quality of the output.

Selecting the printer and/or settings

Just before you're ready to print a document, pull down the File menu and click Document Properties, Print Setup. Now do the following:

1 Click here; select the printer you want from the list

3 Click here

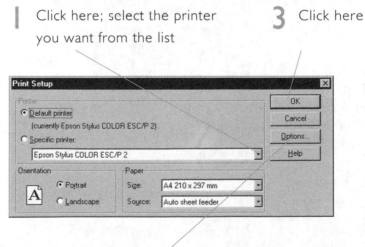

2 To adjust the printer settings, click here and complete the dialog which launches (for how to do this, see your printer's manual)

Customised printing

Once the active document is how you want it (and you've customised the print setup appropriately), the next stage is to print it out. Word Pro makes this process easy and lets you set a variety of options before you do so. These include:

- the number of copies you want printed;

- whether you want the copies 'collated' (one full copy printed at a time). For instance, if you're printing three copies of a 40-page document, Word Pro prints pages 1–40 of the first document, followed by pages 1–40 of the second and pages 1–40 of the third, and;

- only printing odd or even pages.

Starting to print

Pull down the File menu and click Print. Now carry out steps 1–4 below, as appropriate.

Re step 1 – the Collate option is only available in multi-page documents.

Re step 2 – this prints a *single* page range. To print multiple ranges, click the Select Pages button. Do the following:

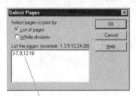

Type in page ranges (eg, 3–7, 9, 12–18) and click OK. Now follow step 4 to begin printing.

To print the last page first, click Options. In the Print Options dialog, click 'In reverse order'.

4 Click here to initiate printing

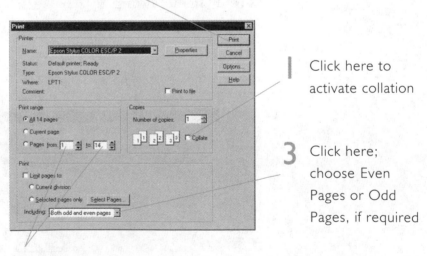

| Click here to activate collation

3 Click here; choose Even Pages or Odd Pages, if required

2 Type in start and end pages

After step 4, Word Pro starts printing the active document.

1-2-3

Chapter Three

This chapter gives you the fundamentals of using 1-2-3. You'll learn how to work with data and formulas, and how to move around through worksheets. You'll also learn how to make your data more visually effective with the use of charts. Finally, you'll customise page layout/printing.

Covers

The 1-2-3 screen

Below is a detailed illustration of the 1-2-3 screen.

Title bar   Menu bar   Contents box

REMEMBER

This is the Selection Indicator: it displays the current cell reference (location details).

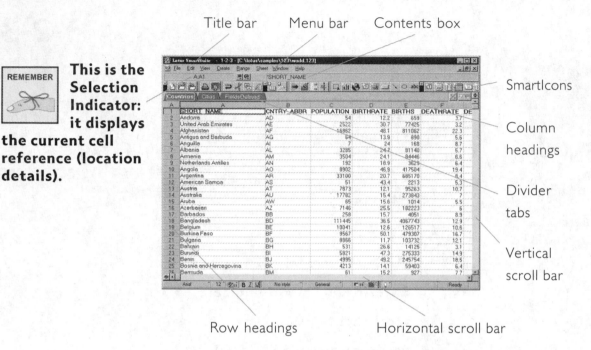

SmartIcons

Column headings

Divider tabs

Vertical scroll bar

Row headings   Horizontal scroll bar

Some of these screen components can be hidden.

Specifying which screen components display

Pull down the View menu and click Set View Preferences. Then do the following:

Click here

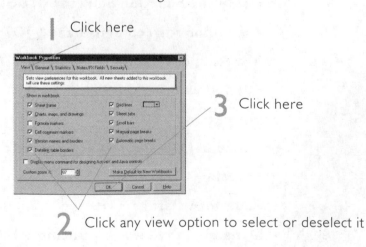

3 Click here

2 Click any view option to select or deselect it

Entering data

When you start 1-2-3, you can use the Welcome screen to produce a new blank worksheet (see Chapter One for how to do this). The result will look something like this:

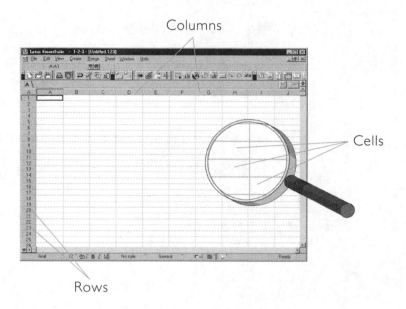

Columns

Cells

Rows

This means that you can start entering data immediately.

In 1-2-3, you can enter the following basic data types:

- values (ie, numbers);

- text (eg, headings and explanatory material);

- functions (eg, Sine or Cosine), and;

- formulas (combinations of values, text and functions).

REMEMBER

Columns are vertical, rows horizontal.

You enter data into 'cells'. Cells are formed where rows and columns intersect – see the illustration above.

Collections of rows/columns and cells are known in 1-2-3 as worksheets. Worksheets are organised into files known as workbooks. Each workbook can have numerous worksheets, if required.

Although you can enter data *directly* into a cell (by simply clicking in it, typing it in and pressing Enter), you can also use another method which is often easier. 1-2-3 provides a special screen component known as the Contents box.

The illustration below shows a section of the worksheet created with the Create an Invoice SmartMaster. Cell C7 is currently flagged in the Selection Indicator.

Selection Indicator

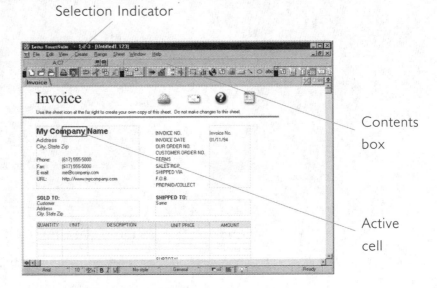

Contents box

Active cell

HANDY TIP

You can use a keyboard route to confirm operations in the Contents box: simply press Return. (To cancel the operation, press Esc instead.)

Entering data via the Contents box

Click the cell you want to insert data into. Then click the Contents box. Type in the data. Then follow step 1 below. If you decide not to proceed with the operation, follow step 2 instead:

Click here

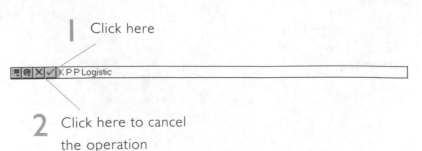

2 Click here to cancel the operation

Modifying existing data

You can amend the contents of a cell in two ways:

- via the Contents box, or;

- from within the cell.

When you use either of these methods, 1-2-3 enters a special state known as Edit Mode.

Amending existing data using the Contents box

Click the cell whose contents you want to change. Then click in the Contents box. Make the appropriate revisions and/or additions. Then press Return. 1-2-3 updates the relevant cell.

Amending existing data internally

Click the cell whose contents you want to change. Press F2. Make the appropriate revisions and/or additions *within the cell*. Then press Return.

The illustration below shows a further section of the worksheet based on the Create an Invoice SmartMaster.

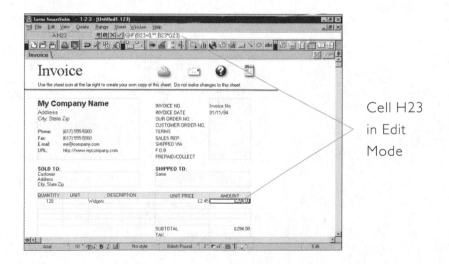

Cell H23 in Edit Mode

Working with cell ranges

When you're working with more than one cell, it's often convenient and useful to organise them in 'ranges'.

A range is a rectangular arrangement of cells. In the illustration below, the following cells have been selected.

C19, C20, D19, D20, E19, E20, F19, F20, G19, G20, H19, H20, I19, I20

See pages 101–102 for how to select cell ranges and rows/columns.

Here, the Selection Indicator shows that the selected range is located in Worksheet A.

A selected cell range

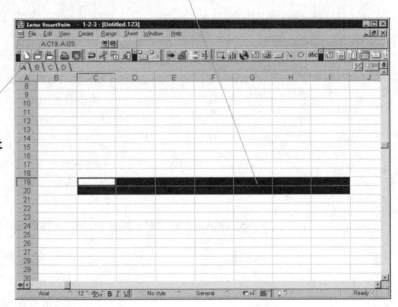

The above description is very cumbersome. It's much more useful to use a form of shorthand. 1-2-3 (using the start and end cells as reference points) refers to these cells as:

C19..I20

This can be extended even more – see the Selection Indicator above – in that cell addresses can also refer to the host worksheet. In this case, our address becomes:

A:C19..A:I20

denoting that the start and end cells are in Worksheet A.

Moving around in worksheets

 Worksheets in the Millennium edition of 1-2-3 can have as many as 65,536 rows.

1-2-3 worksheets are huge. Moving to cells which happen currently to be visible is easy: you simply click in the relevant cell. However, 1-2-3 provides several techniques you can use to jump to less accessible areas.

Using the scroll bars

Use any of the following methods:

1. To scroll quickly to another section of the active worksheet, drag the scroll box along the scroll bar until you reach it.

2. To jump to the left or right, click to the left or right of the scroll box in the horizontal scroll bar.

3. To jump up or down, click above or below the scroll box in the vertical scroll bar.

4. To move up or down by one row, click the appropriate arrow in the vertical scroll bar.

5. To move left or right by one column, click the appropriate arrow in the horizontal scroll bar.

 When you drag the vertical or horizontal scroll box, 1-2-3 displays a box indicating which row or column you're up to:

Row: 12

 You can use your mouse to move to any other worksheet: simply click the appropriate divider tab (see the sample below):

Note that sometimes tabs have names (eg, 'Data').

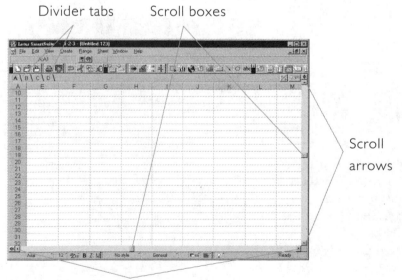

Divider tabs   Scroll boxes

Scroll arrows

Scroll arrows

Using the keyboard

You can use the following techniques:

1. Use the cursor keys to move one cell left, right, up or down.

2. Press Ctrl+↑ to jump left by the number of columns visible, or Ctrl+→ to jump right by the same amount.

3. Press Home to jump to cell A1.

4. Press Page Up or Page Down to move up or down by one screen.

5. Press End+Home to move to the lower right-hand corner of the currently occupied cells.

Using the Go To dialog

1-2-3 provides a special dialog which you can use to specify precise cell destinations (particularly useful in very large worksheets).

Pull down the Edit menu and click Go To. Now do the following:

 In files that host more than one worksheet, use the following:

Ctrl+Page Up — To the next sheet

Ctrl+Page Down — To the previous sheet

 You can use keyboard shortcuts to launch the Go To dialog: simply press:
F5
or
Ctrl+G

 Re step 1 – a cell's 'reference' (or 'address') identifies it in relation to its position in a worksheet – eg, F11 or ß:H23.
  You can also type in cell ranges here.

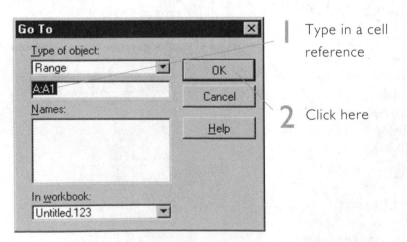

1 Type in a cell reference

2 Click here

Other operations on worksheets

We said earlier that 1-2-3 files can contain numerous worksheets. You can easily:

- add new worksheets;

- delete existing worksheets;

- rename worksheets, or;

- move/copy worksheets (see page 100).

 To rename a worksheet, double-click its tab. Type in the new name and press Return.

Inserting a single worksheet

Right-click the tab that represents the sheet to the right of which you want the new worksheet inserted. In the menu that appears, click Create Sheet. In the Create Sheet dialog, click OK.

Inserting more than one worksheet

To add multiple worksheets, launch the Create Sheet dialog (see above). Then do the following:

 If you want to specify the sheet placement, click one of these options: *before* **step 2.**

 Type in the number of sheets

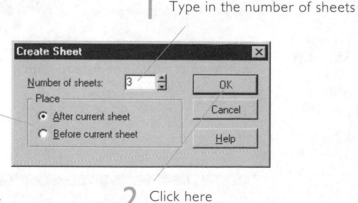

2 Click here

 When you delete a worksheet, note the following:

- 1-2-3 does not launch a warning message – deletion is immediate!

- the worksheet contents are erased, too.

Deleting a worksheet

Right-click the worksheet you want to remove. In the menu that launches, click Delete Sheet.

If you delete a sheet in error, press Ctrl+Z *immediately* to reinstate it.

You can also copy or move sheets, in the following ways:

* with the mouse, or;

* via a dialog.

The mouse route

Move the mouse pointer to the edge of the tab relating to the worksheet you want to move. Do the following:

HANDY TIP

To copy (instead of move) a sheet, hold down Ctrl as you drag.

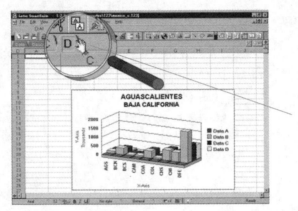

Drag the tab to a new location

REMEMBER

Users of SmartSuite 97 can only use the dialog route.

The dialog route

Pull down the Sheet menu and click Move or Copy Sheet. Do the following:

| Select Move or Copy

3 Click a direction

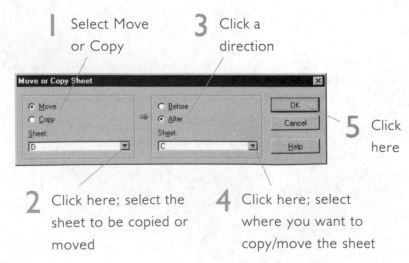

5 Click here

2 Click here; select the sheet to be copied or moved

4 Click here; select where you want to copy/move the sheet

Selection techniques

Before you can carry out any editing operations on cells in 1-2-3, you have to select them first. Selecting a single cell is very easy: you merely click in it. However, 1-2-3 provides a variety of selection techniques which you can use to select more than one cell.

Selecting adjacent cell ranges

The easiest way to do this is to use the mouse. Click in the first cell in the range; hold down the left mouse button and drag over the remaining cells. Release the mouse button.

You can use the keyboard, too. Position the cell pointer over the first cell in the range. Hold down one Shift key as you use the cursor keys to extend the selection. Release the keys when the correct selection has been defined.

Selecting separate cell ranges

1-2-3 lets you select more than one range at a time. Look at the illustration below:

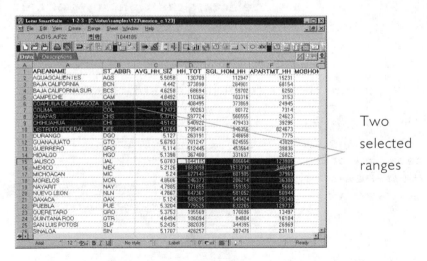

Two selected ranges

To select joint ranges, select the first in the normal way (note that you can't use the F4 method – see the HANDY TIP – for this). Then hold down Ctrl as you select subsequent ranges.

Selecting a single row or column

To select every cell within a row or column automatically, click on the row or column heading.

Clicking here selects the column

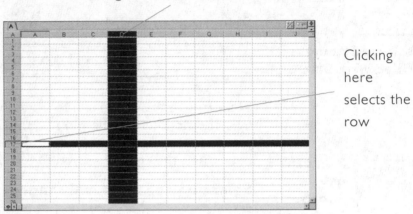

Clicking here selects the row

Selecting multiple rows or columns

To select more than one row/column, click a row or column heading. Hold down the left mouse button and drag over further headings.

Selecting an entire worksheet

HANDY TIP **The Sheet Letter button shows A because worksheet A (as shown in the tab) is active:**

Click the Sheet Letter button:

The Sheet Letter button

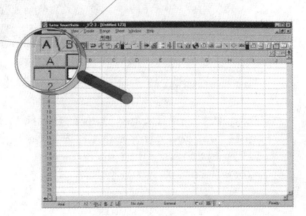

Formulas – an overview

Formulas are cell entries which define how other values relate to each other.

As a very simple example, consider the following:

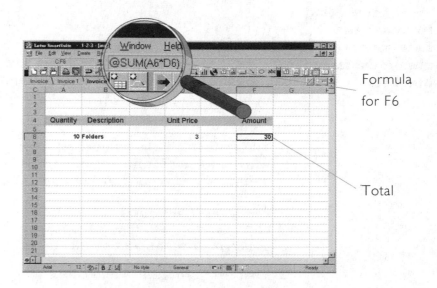

Formula for F6

Total

'@' tells 1-2-3 that a function (in this case, SUM) follows immediately; 'SUM(A6*D6)' tells 1-2-3 to multiply the contents of cells A6 and D6 and display the result.

Here, a cell has been defined which returns the product of the cells A6 and D6. Obviously, in this instance you could insert the total easily enough yourself because the individual values are so small, and because we're only dealing with a small number of cells. But what happens if the cell values are larger and/or more numerous, or – more to the point – if they're liable to change frequently?

The answer is to insert a formula which carries out the necessary calculation automatically.

If you look at the Contents box (magnified in the illustration), you'll see the formula which does this:

@SUM(A6*D6)

Many 1-2-3 formulas are much more complex than this, but the principles remain the same.

Inserting a formula

Arguments (eg, cell references) relating to formulas and functions are always contained in brackets.

Formulas in 1-2-3 contain permutations of the following:

- an operand (cell reference – eg, B4);

- a function (eg, the summation function, SUM);

- an arithmetical operator (+, -, /, * and ^), and;

- comparison operators (<, >, <=, >=, = and <>).

1-2-3 supports a very wide range of functions organised into numerous categories. For more information on how to insert functions, see page 106.

The mathematical operators represent (in the order in which they appear in the bulleted list above): *addition, subtraction, division, multiplication* and *exponentiation*.

The comparison operators are (in the order in which they appear in the list): *less than, greater than, less than or equal to, greater than or equal to, equals* and *not equal to*.

There are two ways to enter formulas:

Entering a formula directly into the cell

Click the cell in which you want to insert a formula. Then type it in – don't forget to surround the argument in brackets. For instance, to add cells H18 and I23, type:

(H18+I23)

When you've finished, press Return.

Entering a formula into the Contents box

Click the cell in which you want to insert a formula. Then click in the Contents box. Type in your formula. When you've finished, press Return or do the following:

Click here

@SUM(B18*F18)

Using SmartLabels

Users of SmartSuite 97 only have access to the 'total' SmartLabel.

1-2-3 makes it even easier to insert formulas. You can use SmartLabels: predefined prompts which automatically insert formulas below or to the right of given ranges. The most commonly used SmartLabels are:

total	—	self-explanatory
subtotal	—	self-explanatory
grandtotal	—	self-explanatory
average	—	returns the average of the row/column
maximum	—	returns the largest entry in the row/column
minimum	—	returns the smallest entry in the row/column

If you want to disable Smart-Labels, pull down the File menu and click User Setup, 1-2-3 Preferences. In the 1-2-3 Preferences dialog, activate the General tab. In the 'Other options:' field, deselect Use SmartLabels to enter formulas and apply formats. Click OK.

Inserting SmartLabels

Type in a SmartLabel prompt:

- (in the case of a row) above and to the right of the relevant range, or;

- (in the case of a column) below and to the left of the relevant range.

You can have as many as 10 blank rows/columns between your SmartLabel and the range it applies to.

8		Jan	Feb	Mar	Total
9	1	12000	45000	12000	69001
10	2	9300	230	11000	20532
11	3	12000	18233	12345	42581

Totalling a row

15		Jan	Feb	Mar
16	1	12000	45000	12000
17	2	9300	230	11000
18	3	12000	18233	12345
19	Total	33300	63463	35345

Totalling a column

Now press Enter in either case to have 1-2-3 enter and activate the relevant formula.

Using the Function Selector

The SUM component of the formula mentioned on page 103 is a function.

Functions are pre-defined tools which accomplish specific tasks. These tasks are often calculations; occasionally, however, they're more generalised (eg, some functions simply return dates and/or times). In effect, functions replace one or more formulas.

1-2-3 provides a special tool to help ensure that you enter functions correctly. This is useful for the following reasons:

Functions are prefixed with '@', and can only be used in formulas.

* 1-2-3 provides so many functions, it's convenient to apply them from a centralised source, and;

* functions must be entered with the correct syntax.

Inserting a function with the Function Selector

At the relevant point in the process of inserting a formula, click the Function Selector button to the left of the Contents box:

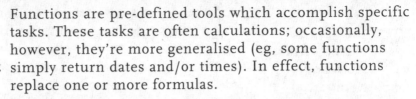

Function Selector button

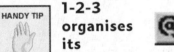

1-2-3 organises its functions under convenient headings, eg:

* Calendar;

* Information;

* Financial, or;

* Text.

If you want to display specific functions in this dialog, click the arrow to the right of the Category field (before you carry out steps 2 and 3) and choose a category.

Now do the following:

 Click here

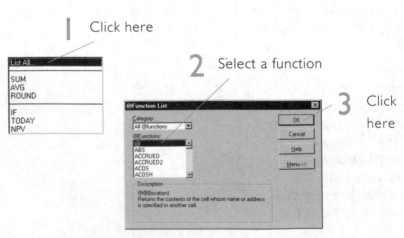

The function is inserted into the cell; complete the arguments as appropriate.

Amending row/column sizes

Sooner or later, you'll find it necessary to change the width of rows or columns. This necessity arises when there is too much data in cells to display adequately. You can enlarge or shrink single or multiple rows/columns.

Changing row height

To change one row's height, click the row heading. If you want to change multiple rows, hold down Ctrl and click the appropriate extra headings. Then place the mouse pointer over the line located just under the row heading(s); it changes to a cross. Hold down the left mouse button and drag the line up or down to decrease or increase the height of the row(s) respectively. Release the mouse button to confirm the operation.

HANDY TIP

1-2-3 has a useful 'best fit' feature. Simply double-click the line below the selected row headings, or to the right of selected column headings, to have the rows or columns adjust themselves automatically to their textual content.

In this magnified view, rows 18 and 19 are being amended

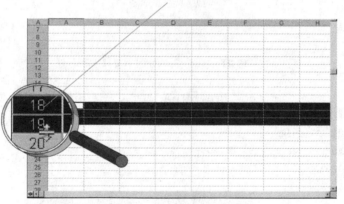

Changing column width

To change one column's width, click the column heading. If you want to change multiple columns, hold down Ctrl and click the appropriate extra headings. Then place the mouse pointer over the line located just to the right of the column heading(s); it changes to a cross. Hold down the left mouse button and drag the line right or left to widen or narrow the column(s) respectively.

Release the mouse button to confirm the operation.

Inserting cells, rows or columns

You can insert additional cells, rows or columns into worksheets.

If you select more than one row or column, 1-2-3 inserts the equivalent number of new rows or columns.

Inserting a new row or column

First, select one or more rows above which you want the new row(s) inserted. Or select one or more columns to the left of which you want the new column(s) inserted. Now pull down the Range menu and click Insert Rows or Insert Columns. 1-2-3 inserts the new row(s) or column(s) immediately.

An extract of a worksheet. Here, four new rows are being added

Inserting a new cell range

Select the range where you want to insert the new cells. Pull down the Range menu and click Insert. Now carry out steps 1–3 below:

This technique inserts a blank range of cells:

- of the same proportions as the selected range, and;
- above or to the left of the selected range.

Click Rows or Columns

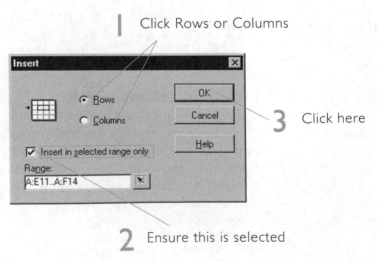

3 Click here

2 Ensure this is selected

Fill by Example

 In the Millennium edition, Fill by Example is more intelligent: it recognises patterns.

For instance, if you type 'October' in one cell and 'J' in the cell below, 1-2-3 inserts:

 January

If this isn't right and you go on to type 'u', 1-2-3 inserts:

June

Press Enter when the correct entry displays.

 You can also work with the following series types:

- numbers (eg, 1, 3, 5, 7);
- letters (eg, A, B, C, D), and;
- days of the week.

1-2-3 lets you insert data series automatically. This is a very useful and time-saving feature. Look at the illustration below:

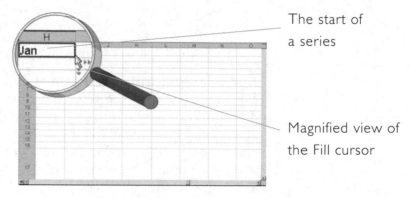

The start of a series

Magnified view of the Fill cursor

If you wanted to insert month names in successive cells in column A, you could do so manually. But there's a much easier way. You can use 1-2-3's Fill by Example feature.

Using Fill by Example to create a series

Type in the first element(s) of the series in consecutive cells. Select the cells you want to fill. Then position the mouse pointer over the bottom right-hand corner of the last cell (the pointer changes – see the illustration above). Hold down the left mouse button and drag over the cells into which you want to extend the series (in the example here, over H2..H12). When you release the mouse button, 1-2-3 extrapolates the initial entry or entries into the appropriate series.

A	H
1	Jan
2	Feb
3	Mar
4	Apr
5	May
6	Jun
7	Jul
8	Aug
9	Sep
10	Oct
11	Nov
12	Dec

The completed series

Changing number formats

1-2-3 lets you apply formatting enhancements to cells and their contents. You can:

- specify a number format;

- customise the font, type size and style of contents, and;

- specify cell alignment.

Specifying a number format

You can customise the way cell contents (eg, numbers and dates/times) display in 1-2-3. For example, you can often specify the number of decimal places which numbers should display. Available formats are organised under several general categories. These include: Currency, Date, Time and Number.

Select the cells whose contents you want to customise. Pull down the Range menu and click Range Properties. Now do the following:

Select this tab

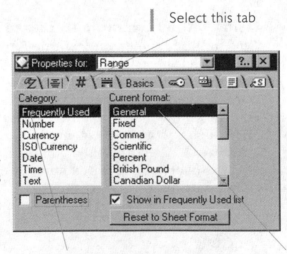

REMEMBER

Re step 3 – the options you can choose from vary according to the category chosen.

2 Click a category

3 Select a format

Changing fonts and attributes

1-2-3 lets you carry out the following actions on cell contents (numbers and/or text):

- apply a new font and/or type size;

- apply a font attribute (for most fonts, you can choose from Normal, Italic, Bold or Underline, although other possibilities include Dbl underline, Wide underline and Strikethrough), and;

- apply a colour.

Amending the appearance of cell contents

Select the cell(s) whose contents you want to reformat. Pull down the Range menu and click Range Properties. Follow step 1, and then any of steps 2–5, as appropriate:

| Click here | 2 Click the font you want to use | 3 Enter the type size you need |

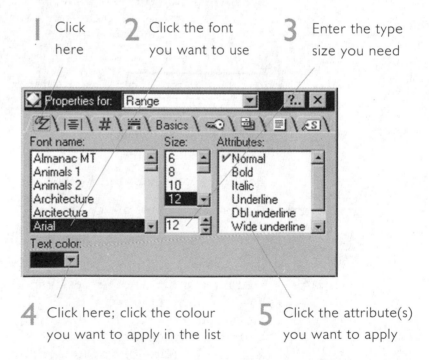

4 Click here; click the colour you want to apply in the list

5 Click the attribute(s) you want to apply

Cell alignment

By default, 1-2-3 aligns text to the left of cells, and numbers to the right. However, if you want you can change this.

You can specify alignment under two broad headings: Horizontal and Vertical.

Horizontal alignment
The main options are:

General the default (see above)

Left contents are aligned from the left

Center contents are centred

Right contents are aligned from the right

Evenly Spaced contents are separated by spaces so that they fill the cell – see the cell in the example below:

 A cell with Evenly Spaced alignment

Vertical alignment
Available options are:

Top contents align with the top of the cell(s)

Center contents are centred

Bottom contents align with the cell bottom

Most of these settings parallel features found in Word Pro (and many other word processors). The difference, however, lies in the fact that 1-2-3 has to align data within the bounds of cells rather than a page. When it aligns text, it often needs to employ its own version of text wrap. See page 113 for more information on this.

You can also specify an orientation for cell contents – see page 113.

Other alignment features you can set are orientation and text wrap.

Orientation controls the direction of text flow within cells; there are several available options, expressed visually in the Orientation field (see the REMEMBER tip below).

When the Wrap text option is selected, 1-2-3 – instead of overflowing any surplus text into adjacent cells to the right – forces it onto separate lines within the host cell.

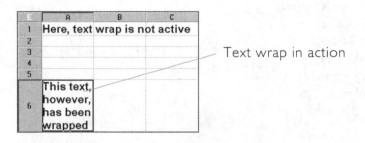

Text wrap in action

Customising cell alignment

Select the cell(s) whose contents you want to realign. Pull down the Range menu and click Range Properties. Carry out step 1 below. Now follow steps 2–4, as appropriate.

Re step 4 – choose an orientation from the following drop-down list:

1 Select this tab

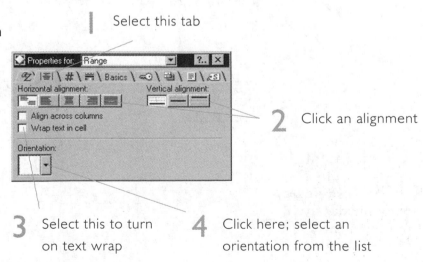

2 Click an alignment

3 Select this to turn on text wrap

4 Click here; select an orientation from the list

Using the Gallery

1-2-3 provides a shortcut to the formatting of worksheet data: the Gallery.

REMEMBER

The Gallery schemes are in fact graphics styles.

The Gallery consists of 14 pre-defined formatting schemes. These incorporate specific excerpts from several of the formatting options that were discussed earlier; additionally, a few incorporate three-dimensional components for increased visual effect. You can apply any of these schemes (and their associated formatting) to selected cell ranges with just a few mouse clicks.

BEWARE

The Gallery works with most arrangements of data. However, some may require a certain amount of manual adjustment first...

Applying preset formatting

First, select the cell range you want to apply an automatic format to. Pull down the Range menu and click Range Properties. Now carry out steps 1–4 below:

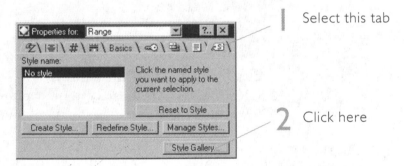

1 Select this tab

2 Click here

3 Click a formatting scheme

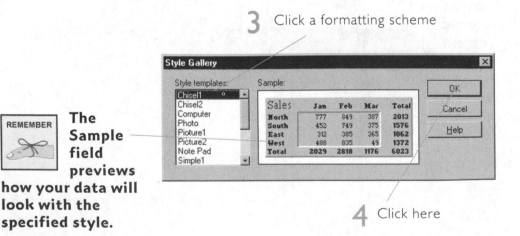

REMEMBER

The Sample field previews how your data will look with the specified style.

4 Click here

Find operations

1-2-3 lets you search for and jump to text or numbers (in short, any information) in your worksheets. This is a particularly useful feature when worksheets become large and complex, as they almost invariably do.

You can specify whether 1-2-3 looks in:

- cells which contain text ('labels');

- cells which don't contain formulas;

- cells which contain text *and* those which contain formulas, or;

- all open worksheets (or simply a pre-selected cell range – see the REMEMBER tip).

Re step 2 – if you want to restrict the search to specific cells, select a cell range before you launch the Find and Replace dialog. This automatically activates the Selected range option.

Searching for data

Pull down the Edit menu and click Find & Replace. Now carry out step 1 below, then either or both of steps 2 and 3. Finally, carry out step 4.

| Type in the data you want to find

4 Click here

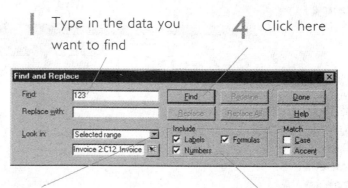

2 Click here; select a search definition in the list

3 Define the types of cells searched

If you want a case-specific search, select Case in the Match section before you follow step 4.

When you've finished with the Find and Replace dialog, click this button:

Find-and-replace operations

When you search for data, you can also have 1-2-3 replace it with something else. You can have this done automatically, or you can have 1-2-3 request your confirmation before making the exchange.

As with find operations, you can specify whether 1-2-3 looks in cells which contain text, cells which contain formulas, or both. You can also have 1-2-3 search through all active worksheets, or through selected cell ranges.

Re step 3 – if you want to restrict the find-and-replace operation to specific cells, select a cell range before you launch the Find and Replace dialog. This automatically activates the Selected range option.

Running a find-and-replace operation

Pull down the Edit menu and click Find & Replace. Carry out steps 1 and 2, then 3 and/or 4, as appropriate. Follow step 5 to replace only *one* flagged instance of the search data (repeat as often as necessary). Alternatively, follow step 6 to replace *all* instances.

1 Type in the data you want to find

2 Type in the replacement data

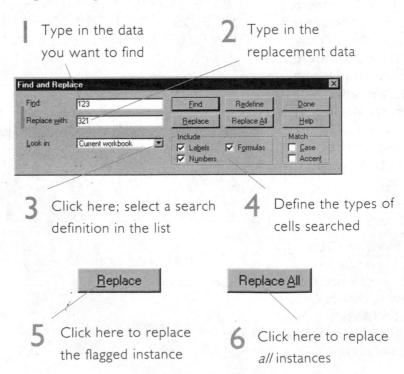

When you've finished with the Find and Replace dialog, click the Done button to close it.

3 Click here; select a search definition in the list

4 Define the types of cells searched

5 Click here to replace the flagged instance

6 Click here to replace *all* instances

The buttons shown on the right are excerpts from the Find and Replace dialog.

Charting

1-2-3 has comprehensive charting capabilities. You can have it convert selected data into its visual equivalent. To do this, 1-2-3 offers a wide number of chart formats and sub-formats.

Creating a chart

Select the cells you want to convert into a chart. Pull down the Create menu and click Chart. The cursor becomes:

You can have 1-2-3 create charts in worksheets which do not host the source data.

Hold down the left mouse button and drag to define the area into which you want the new chart inserted:

Select the appropriate cells in one worksheet. Click Chart in the Create menu, then click the tab for the second worksheet *immediately*. Define the catchment area for the chart in the second worksheet, then release the mouse button.

Catchment area for chart

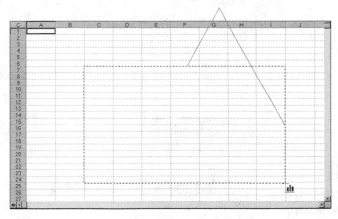

When you release the button, 1-2-3 inserts the chart.

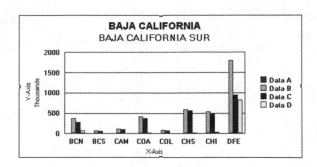

...cont'd

By default, 1-2-3 creates simple bar charts. However, you can easily apply a new chart type if you want.

You can choose from 12 overall chart types. These include:

- Line;

- Area;

- Pie;

- 3D versions of the above, and;

- Radar.

Many of these are further divided into sub-types.

Applying a new chart type

To change the chart type, do the following. Select the chart by clicking its frame. Pull down the Chart menu and click Chart Type. Now do the following:

REMEMBER

Re step 3 – the 1-2-3 sub-types provide a lot of variety.
Note, however, that some chart types – XY (Scatter) and Number Grid – do not have associated sub-types.

Select this tab

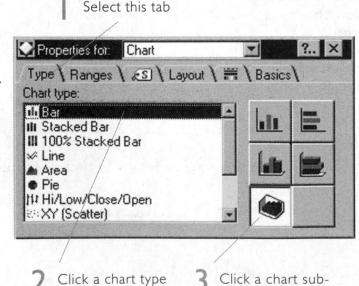

2 Click a chart type

3 Click a chart sub-type, if applicable

Page setup issues

HANDY TIP

To set the paper size, click this tab in the Infobox:

Then click the arrow to the right of the Paper size field. In the list which launches, select the paper size you want to use.

Making sure your worksheets print with the correct page setup can be a complex issue, for the simple reason that most worksheets become very extensive with the passage of time (so large, in fact, that in the normal course of things they won't fit onto a single page).

Page setup features you can customise include:

*   the paper orientation;

*   scaling;

*   margins (Top, Bottom, Left and Right), and;

*   the centring of data.

Setting page options

Pull down the File menu and click Preview & Page Setup. Now do the following, as appropriate:

HANDY TIP

The current worksheet is displayed in this tiled window on the left:

HANDY TIP

Changes you make to the worksheet layout are mirrored in the Preview window.

REMEMBER

Re step 4 – you can centre print data vertically, horizontally or both.

1 Click an orientation   2 Adjust these margin settings

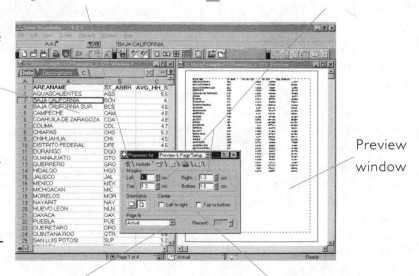

Preview window

3 Click here; choose a scaling option   4 Select a centre alignment

Launching Dynamic Preview

1-2-3 provides a special view mode called Dynamic Preview. This displays the active worksheet (exactly as it will look when printed) in a special window called the Preview window. Alongside this is a window showing the normal worksheet view. Use Dynamic Preview as a final check just before you begin printing.

You can perform the following actions from within Dynamic Preview:

- move from page to page;

- zoom in or out on the active page;

- display more than one page;

- adjust Page Setup options (see page 119), and;

- begin printing. .

REMEMBER

To specify which pages are previewed, click this tab:

Click Pages. In the From: and To: fields, type in start and end pages.

Launching Dynamic Preview
Pull down the File menu and click Preview & Page Setup. The Preview window now launches, together with the Preview & Page Setup Infobox. To determine which worksheet sections are previewed, carry out steps 1–2 below:

Select this tab

REMEMBER

Re the above tip – users of SmartSuite 97 should carry out a different procedure.
Follow step 1. In the From: and To: fields in the Pages section, type in start and end pages.

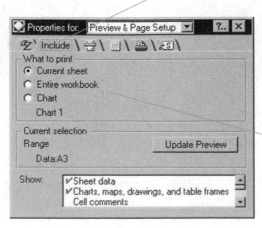

2 Define the Preview area

Using Dynamic Preview

 The icon which hides margins is unavailable in SmartSuite 97.

 In the Preview window, use the scroll bars to move to parts of your worksheet which aren't currently visible.

 Users of the Millennium edition can manipulate margins directly in the Preview window.

Move the magnifying cursor over a margin line; it changes to:

Drag the margin in or out. As you do so, a helpful box gives a progress report:

Left Margin: 1.572 cm

Release the mouse button to confirm the change.

All of the operations you can undertake in Dynamic Preview can be accessed from the overhead SmartIcons.

Click any of the following buttons, as appropriate:

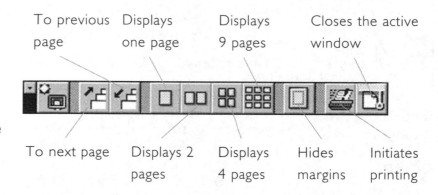

To previous page Displays one page Displays 9 pages Closes the active window

To next page Displays 2 pages Displays 4 pages Hides margins Initiates printing

Using Zoom

To zoom in within the Preview window, move the mouse pointer:

anywhere in the window. Then do the following, as appropriate:

1. Left-click once to zoom in (increase the magnification).

2. Left-click again to further increase the magnification.

3. Left-click again to return to the standard view.

Closing the Preview window

When you've finished using the Preview window, click this button in the top right-hand corner:

X

Printing worksheet data

1-2-3 lets you specify:

- the number of copies you want printed;

- which pages (or page ranges) you want printed, and;

- whether you want the print run restricted to cells you selected before initiating printing.

You can 'mix and match' these, as appropriate.

Starting a print run

Open the file which contains the data you want to print. If you want to print an entire worksheet, click the relevant divider tab. Alternatively, if you need to print a specific cell range within a worksheet, select it. Then pull down the File menu and click Print. Do any of steps 1–3. Then carry out step 4 to begin printing:

You can use a keyboard shortcut to launch the Print dialog.
Simply press Ctrl+P.

Click here to preview your data – and/or adjust the page setup options – *before* printing (see pages 119–121 for how to do so).

2 Type in start and end page numbers

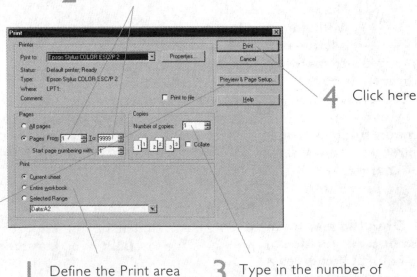

4 Click here

| Define the Print area

3 Type in the number of copies you require

Approach

This chapter gives you the fundamentals of using Approach. You'll learn how to select/work with data; use formulas/functions; move around in databases; and interact with data in views. You'll also learn how to locate/replace data, and enhance formatting in forms. Finally, you'll customise page layout/printing.

Covers

Chapter Four

The Approach screen

Below is a detailed illustration of a typical Approach screen.

Title bar   Menu bar

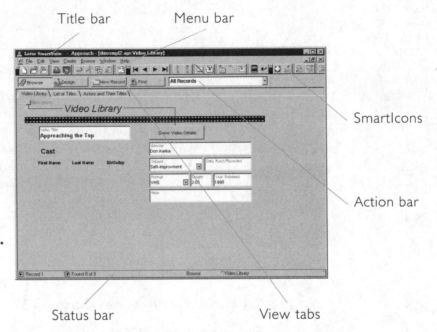

REMEMBER

This is a database form (it displays only one record at a time).

For more information on forms, see page 129.

SmartIcons

Action bar

Status bar   View tabs

Some of these – eg, the Title and Menu bars – are standard to just about all programs which run under Windows. Other components can be hidden at will.

Specifying which screen components display

Pull down the File menu; click User Setup, Approach Preferences. Then do the following:

Click here

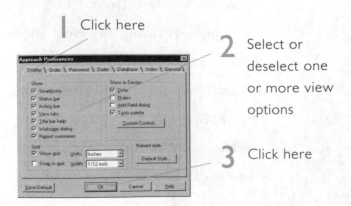

2 Select or deselect one or more view options

3 Click here

Creating your first database

The procedures described here help you create a blank database and then insert your own fields. If, however, any of the database types shown here: approximate to the database you want to create, you may find it preferable to use them.

Simply select a SmartMaster in step 1. Then follow step 2. Approach creates your database immediately.

We saw in Chapter One how to create new blank documents in the main SmartSuite modules. Approach, however, has certain refinements. We'll look at the process in more detail here.

To create a new database from within Approach, pull down the File menu and click New Database. Do the following:

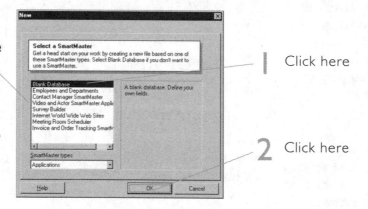

1 Click here

2 Click here

Pages 125–126 amplify the instructions given on page 16.

3 Click here. In the drop-down list, click the drive/folder you want to host the database

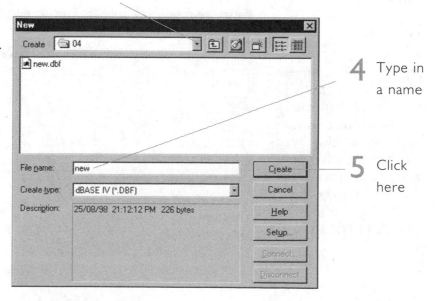

4 Type in a name

5 Click here

...cont'd

The next stage is to define the fields you want your new database to have. Carry out step 6 below:

6 Type in a field name

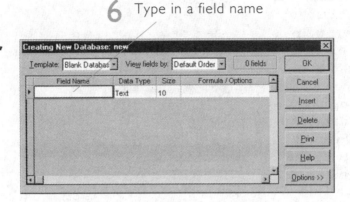

 In Approach, data is entered into individual fields. (For more information on fields, see pages 127–128.)

 Internally, databases consist of several constituent files (but Approach manages these for you).

Now press Return. Repeat this procedure for as many fields as you need (you can, of course, add additional fields later, if required). The completed dialog will look something like this:

7 Click here

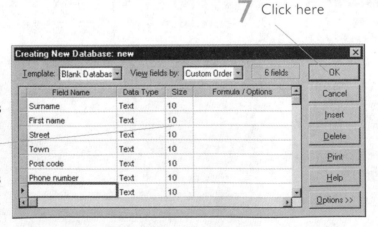

The entries in the Size column: determine the size of the fields (and therefore how much information can be inserted).
  It's a good idea to increase the default now.

Follow step 7 when you've entered enough fields. Approach creates the new database.

Entering data

When you've created a database, you can begin entering data immediately. You can enter the following basic data types:

- numbers;
- text;
- functions, and;
- formulas (combinations of numbers, text and functions).

 You can enter data into the following:

- worksheets, and;
- forms.

In worksheets, records are shown as single, horizontal rows.
In forms, on the other hand, only one record displays on-screen at any given time.
(For more information on forms/worksheets see page 129.)

 This is a worksheet. Database worksheets are suitable for the mass insertion of data; if applicable (it isn't here), more than 1 record is visible at a time.

You enter data into 'fields'. Fields are organised into 'records'. Records are whole units of related information.

To understand this, we'll take a specific example. In an address book, the categories under which information is entered (eg, 'Surname', 'Address', 'Phone No.') are fields, while each person whose details are entered into the database constitutes one record. The next illustration (this is one aspect of the database we created on pages 125–126) demonstrates this:

Fields

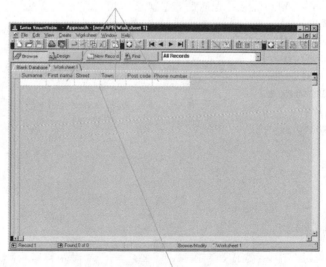

Here, all six fields constitute one record

...cont'd

You can enter data *directly* into a database field. You can do this in both forms and worksheets (with the same technique – but see the REMEMBER tip).

In the illustration below, data is being entered into a form:

You must be in Browse mode to enter or amend data (see page 129).

Click a field, then
begin entering data

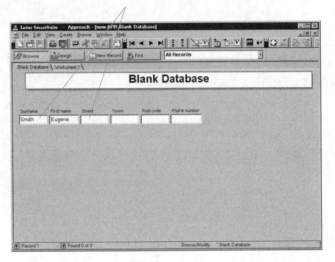

To replace existing data, click in the relevant field. Make the necessary substitution, then press Enter.
For more accuracy in worksheets, double-click a field. Move the insertion point to the correct location, then make the necessary changes. Finally, press Enter.

Press Enter to confirm the operation. Repeat this procedure for as many fields as necessary.

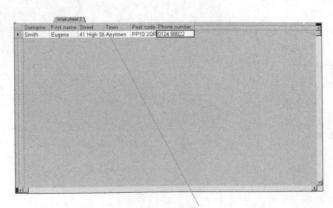

The completed record viewed in a worksheet

Using Browse mode

There is another way in which you can interact with Approach: Design mode.

This mostly relates to forms rather than worksheets, and will be discussed in later topics.

Most of your work in Approach will be done in Browse mode. Browse mode is used for editing data; you do this by using two further database components: forms and worksheets.

Forms

Forms display only one record at a time, while presenting it in a way that is more visual and therefore easier on the eye. The form is the underlying database layout, which you can customise in Design mode. In many circumstances, Forms provide the best way to interact with your database.

Worksheets

Worksheets present data in a grid structure reminiscent of 1-2-3, with the vertical columns denoting fields and the horizontal rows individual records. Pictures and many formatting components do not display. Use worksheets for *bulk* data entry.

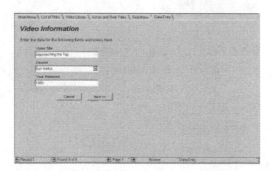

A form from a database created with the Video and Actor SmartMaster

Worksheets are not created in this SmartMaster – for how to generate your own, see page 140.

A worksheet from the same database

Switching between modes

You can use three methods to switch between Browse and Design modes.

The menu route

Pull down the View menu and do the following:

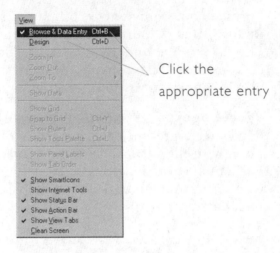

Click the
appropriate entry

The Action bar route

Make sure the Action bar is visible. (If it isn't, pull down the View menu and click Show Action Bar.) Now do one of the following:

Click here to enter Design Mode

Click here to enter Browse mode

The keyboard route

Use any of the following combinations:

Ctrl+B   Browse mode

Ctrl+D   Design mode

Moving around in databases

Like worksheets in 1-2-3, databases can quickly become very large.

Approach provides several techniques you can use to find your way around.

Using the scroll bars
Use any of the following methods:

1. To scroll quickly to another record in worksheets, drag the vertical scroll box along the scroll bar until it's visible. To reach another field in forms, drag the horizontal scroll box until it's visible.

2. To move one window to the left or right (in both worksheets and forms), click to the left or right of the scroll box in the horizontal scroll bar.

3. To move one window up or down (in both worksheets and forms), click above or below the scroll box in the vertical scroll bar.

4. To move left or right by one field in worksheets, click the arrows in the horizontal scroll bar.

Scroll boxes

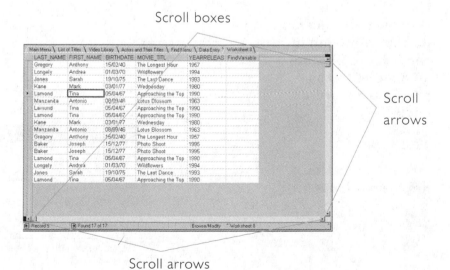

Scroll arrows

Scroll arrows

...cont'd

Using the keyboard
You can use the following techniques:

1. In worksheets, use the cursor keys to move one field left, right, up or down. Or press Tab to move to the adjoining field on the right (Shift+Tab reverses the direction).

2. In forms, press Tab to move to the next field (again, Shift+Tab reverses the direction).

3. In forms and worksheets, press Ctrl+Home to move to the first record in the open database, or Ctrl+End to move to the last.

4. In worksheets, press Page Up or Page Down to move up or down by one screen.

5. In forms, press Page Down to view the next record, or Page Up to view the previous one.

HANDY TIP

Re step 1 – this is the Record button in the Status bar at the base of the screen. You can also do the following in the Record button:
To move to the previous record, click:

To move to the next record, click:

Using the Go to Record dialog
Approach provides a special dialog that you can use to specify which record you want to view. Do the following:

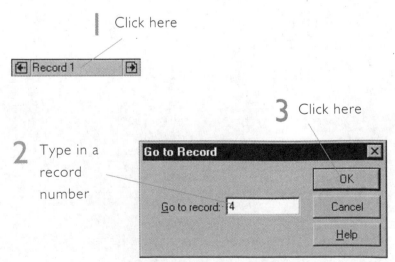

Click here

2 Type in a record number

3 Click here

Using Zoom

The ability to vary the level of magnification in Approach is very useful. Sometimes, it's helpful to 'zoom out' (ie, decrease the magnification) so that you can take an overview; at other times, you'll need to 'zoom in' (increase the magnification) to work in greater detail. Approach makes this process easy and convenient.

You can change magnification levels in Approach:

- from within the View menu, or;

- by using the Zoom button in the Status bar.

You can only use Zoom in forms, in Design mode.

Using the View menu
Pull down the View menu. Now do the following:

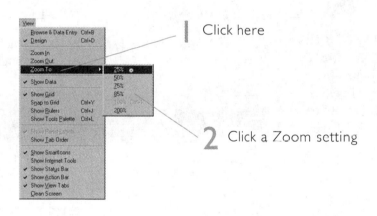

Click here

2 Click a Zoom setting

Using the Zoom button
Do the following:

2 Click a Zoom setting

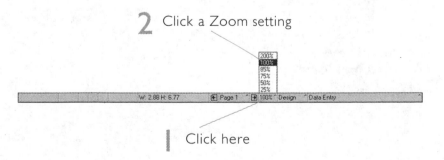

Click here

Selection techniques in worksheets

Before you can carry out any editing operations on fields or records in Approach, you have to select them first. The available selection techniques vary according to whether you're currently using a worksheet or form.

Follow any of the techniques below:

A range is an oblong block/ selection of fields.

To select a single field	simply click in it
To select multiple fields	click the field in the top left-hand corner of the range you want to select; hold down the mouse button and drag over the fields you want to highlight. Release the mouse button.
To select one record	click the record header
To select multiple records	hold down Shift as you click the relevant record headers:

With the exception of the first, selected fields are filled with black.

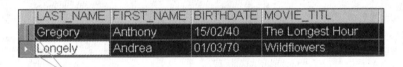

Record headers

To select all data within the active worksheet	carry out step 1 below:

To select all columns and rows (but not the data they contain), perform step 1 again.

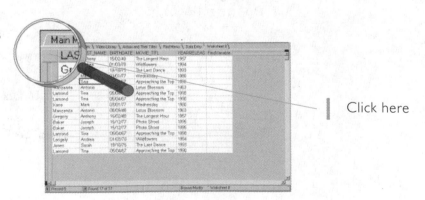

Click here

Selection techniques in forms

Using the mouse

To select a single field   simply click in it

To select multiple fields   hold down Shift as you click in successive fields (you must be in Design mode to do this)

Note that some of the techniques discussed here (they're clearly marked) will only work in Design mode.

To select one record   use the Record button in the Status bar (for how to do this, see page 132)

To select inserted pictures   In Design mode, hold down Shift as you click on successive pictures

To insert a picture into a form, ensure you're in Design mode. Pull down the Edit menu and click Picture, Import. In the Import Picture dialog, locate and select the graphic you want to use. Click OK.

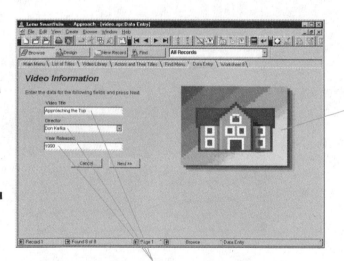

Inserted image

Fields

Using the keyboard

To select a record   Press Page Up or Page Down until the record you want is displayed

Formulas – an overview

You can insert formulas into Approach databases, but only in worksheets. Formulas in Approach work in (very broadly) the same way as in 1-2-3. However, there are certain stipulations:

• you can only insert formulas into whole columns (rather than into individual fields), and;

• as a result of the above, formulas can only apply to data in rows (records), although you can omit specific fields (by not including them).

Look at the next illustration:

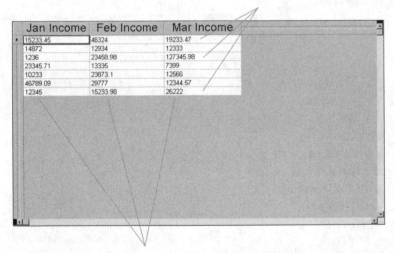

In Approach, you can total rows (records)...

Jan Income	Feb Income	Mar Income
15233.45	46324	19233.47
14872	12934	12333
1236	23458.98	127345.98
23345.71	13335	7399
10233	23873.1	12566
46789.09	29777	12344.57
12345	15233.98	26222

...but not individual fields (columns)

For instance, in the above example you can insert a column which automatically totals the data in all 7 horizontal rows/ records (or only the data in specific fields within all the records), but it isn't possible to total the individual vertical columns.

Inserting a formula

As in 1-2-3, Approach formulas are usually followed by a permutation of the following:

- one or more operands (in the case of Approach, field names);

- a function (eg, AVG – returns the Average), or;

- an arithmetical operator (eg, +, -, /, * and ^).

Approach supports a very wide assortment of functions. For information on how to insert functions, refer to page 138.

The arithmetical operators are (in the order in which they appear in the bulleted list above):

plus, minus, divide, multiply and *exponential.*

Formulas can only be entered in one (highly specific) two-stage process.

Creating a formula column

In a worksheet, move the mouse pointer over the header of the column to the right of which you want the formula column inserted. The pointer changes to a wedge:

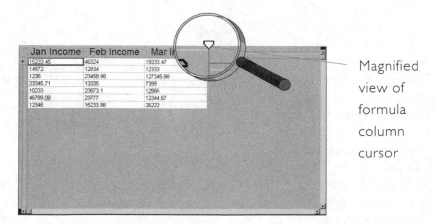

Magnified view of formula column cursor

Left-click once.

...cont'd

When the red cross disappears from the flag, the syntax of your formula is workable (though not necessarily complete).

Re step 2 – to enter a function instead, click an entry in this field:
Complete the syntax in the Formula box, then follow step 3.

If you close the Formula dialog without specifying the correct formula/function, Approach inserts the new (empty) column. To relaunch the dialog, move the mouse pointer over the header of the column to the left and click the wedge. Complete the dialog as appropriate.

The next stage in inserting a formula is the completion of the Formula dialog.

Carry out steps 1 and 2 below as often as necessary. (In this particular example, you need to carry out step 1 in respect of all three fields, and step 2 twice). Finally, carry out step 3 when you've finished:

1 Double-click a field

3 Click here

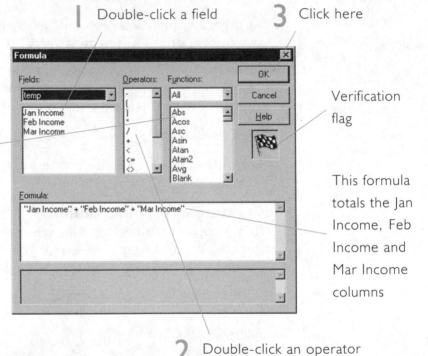

Verification flag

This formula totals the Jan Income, Feb Income and Mar Income columns

2 Double-click an operator

After step 3, Approach inserts the formula column:

Jan Income	Feb Income	Mar Income	
15233.45	46324	19233.47	80790.92
14872	12934	12333	40139
1236	23458.98	127345.98	152040.96
23345.71	13335	7399	44079.71
10233	23873.1	12566	46672.1
46789.09	29777	12344.57	88910.66
12345	15233.98	26222	53800.98

Formula column

Creating new forms

Approach lets you create new forms in your databases.

Pull down the Create menu and click Form. Now do the following:

1 Name the new form   2 Click a layout

The Sample Form field provides a preview of what your form will look like.

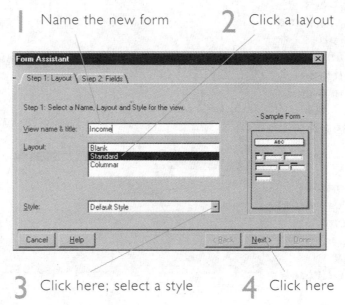

3 Click here; select a style   4 Click here

5 Click a field   6 Click here

Repeat steps 5 and 6 for as many fields as you want to add to the new form. Then carry out step 7.

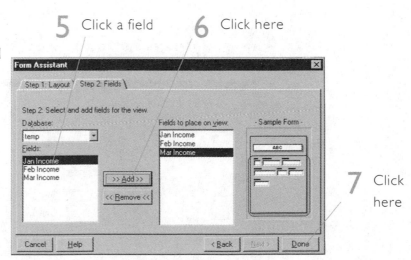

7 Click here

Creating new worksheets

Approach lets you create new worksheets in your databases.

Pull down the Create menu and click Worksheet. Now do the following:

Repeat steps 1 and 2 for as many fields as you want to add to the new worksheet. Then carry out step 3.

The Sample Worksheet field provides a preview of what your worksheet will look like.

1 Click a field

2 Click here

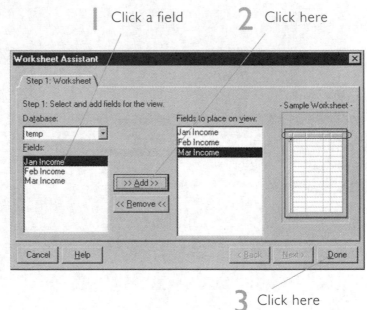

3 Click here

Approach creates and inserts the new worksheet:

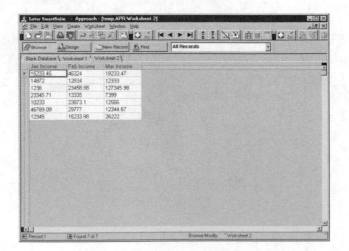

Creating/inserting new fields

You can launch this dialog from within forms in Browse mode – however, Approach automatically switches to Design mode.

You can add one or more blank fields to the active database, from within forms (in Design mode) or worksheets (in Browse or Design mode). Once created, fields can be inserted into the database.

Pull down the Create menu and click Field Definition. Do the following:

1 Click the blank field at the base of the current fields; type in a name for the new field

When you follow step 1, Approach creates another blank field below the new one: Ignore this unless you want to create a further field.

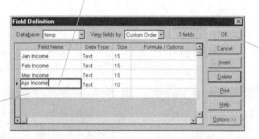

2 Click here

3 Click the new field; drag it to where you want it placed

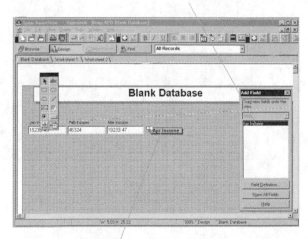

4 When the field is in the correct location, release the button

Inserting a record

If the Action bar isn't on-screen, pull down the View menu and click Show Action Bar.

You can add blank records to the active database from within forms or worksheets (but not if you're working with a form in Design mode).

Refer to the Action bar at the top of the screen and do the following:

Click here

There's a keyboard shortcut you can use here to create and insert a new record: simply press Ctrl+N.

Approach now creates and inserts the new record.

The illustration below shows a new record in a form.

If you want to abort new record creation before you've entered any data, simply press Esc.
Or press Page Up or Page Down, as appropriate, to view an existing record.

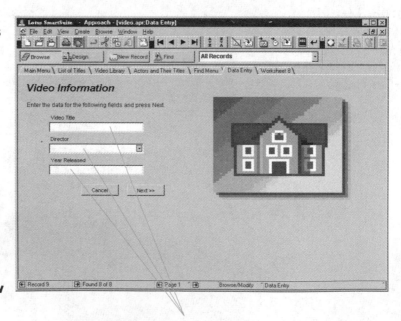

Fields in the new record

Complete the new fields in the usual way.

Amending record/field sizes

To select more than one record header, hold down Shift as you click them.

Sooner or later, you'll find it necessary to change the dimensions of fields or records within worksheets. This necessity arises when there is too much data to display adequately. You can enlarge or shrink all records within a worksheet, or individual columns/fields.

Changing record height

To change the height of all records within a worksheet, move the mouse pointer over any record header. The pointer changes to a double-headed cross. Click and hold down the left mouse button; drag the records down to enlarge them, or up to shrink them.

These are row headers:

Jan Income	Feb Income	Mar Income	Total
15233.45	46324	19233.47	80790.92
14872	12934	12333	40139
1236	23458.98	127345.98	152040.96
23345.71	13335	7399	44079.71
10233	23873.1	12566	46672.1
46789.09	29777	12344.57	88910.66
12345	15233.98	26222	53800.98

Records whose height has been increased

Changing field widths

To change one field/column's width, click the header. If you want to change multiple fields, hold down Shift and click the appropriate extra headers. Then move the mouse pointer over the left or right header edge. Drag inwards to shrink the fields, or outwards to enlarge them.

Column headers

Jan Income	Feb Income	Mar Income	Total
15233.45	46324	19233.47	80790.92
14872	12934	12333	40139
1236	23458.98	127345.98	152040.96
23345.71	13335	7399	44079.71
10233	23873.1	12566	46672.1
46789.09	29777	12344.57	88910.66
12345	15233.98	26222	53800.98

All 4 columns have been resized

Changing fonts and attributes

In forms in Design mode, Approach lets you apply the following actions to field contents (numbers, text or combinations of both):

- a new font;

- a new type size;

- alignment;

- a font attribute (*Italic*, **Bold**, <u>Underline</u> or ~~Strikethrough~~), and;

- a colour.

To select multiple fields, hold down Shift as you click them.

If more than one field is selected, the Field Object menu becomes the Multiple Objects menu.

Amending field contents

Select the field/data you want to reformat. Pull down the Field Object menu and click Object Properties. Carry out step 1 below. Now follow any of steps 2–6, as appropriate.

1 Click this tab   2 Click a font   3 Enter a type size

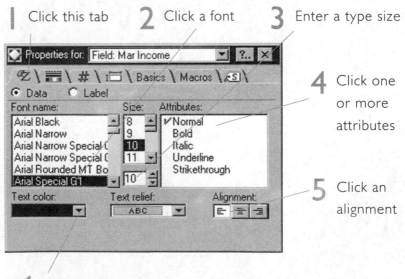

4 Click one or more attributes

5 Click an alignment

6 Click here; select a colour from the list

Bordering fields

REMEMBER

The baseline is the imaginary line on which text (excluding 'descenders' – the lowest points of letters like 'p' and 'q') sits:

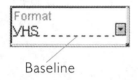

Baseline

REMEMBER

To select multiple fields, hold down Shift as you click them. (If more than one field is selected, the Field Object menu becomes the Multiple Objects menu.)

HANDY TIP

Select this: to display the text baseline.

In forms in Design mode, you can define and customise a border around one or more fields (to select more than one field, hold down the Shift key as you click them). You can specify:

- which sides are bordered;

- whether you want the text baseline shown;

- the border colour;

- the border thickness, and;

- a preset border style.

Applying a field border

First, select the field/data you want to reformat. Pull down the Field Object menu and click Object Properties. Carry out step 1 below. Then follow steps 2–5, as appropriate:

1 Ensure this tab is active

2 Click here; select a style from the list

3 Click one or more border options

4 Click here; select a colour from the list

5 Click here; select a width from the list

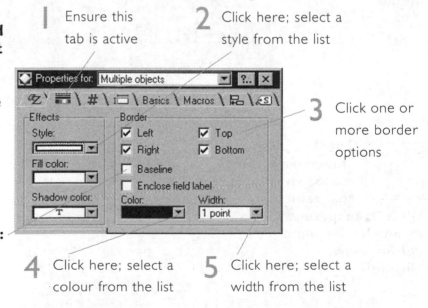

Shading fields

In forms in Design mode, you can apply the following to one or more fields:

- a fill colour, and;
- a shadow colour.

To select multiple fields, hold down Shift as you click them.

Applying a fill and/or shadow colour

First, select the field/data you want to reformat. Pull down the Field Object menu and click Object Properties. Carry out step 1 below. Then follow step 2 and/or 3. Finally, perform step 4 in either case:

If more than one field is selected, the Field Object menu becomes the Multiple Objects menu.

I Ensure this tab is active

2 Click here

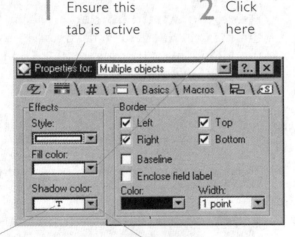

3 Click here

The 'T' shown here means that the field fill is 'transparent': ie, any background colour shows through.

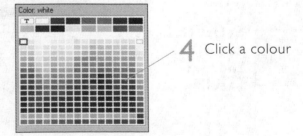

4 Click a colour

Find operations

You must be in Browse mode to carry out Find operations.

Approach lets you search for text and/or numbers in forms and worksheets. You can:

- limit the search to a specific selection;

- (in forms) limit the search specifically to the active record;

- make the search case-sensitive (eg, searching for 'March' would not flag 'march'), and;

- search for the whole field (eg, searching for 'part' would not flag 'party' or 'partly').

Searching for data

Pull down the Edit menu and click Find & Replace Text. Follow step 1 below. Carry out steps 2 and 3, if applicable. Now follow step 4. To find further instances of the search data, carry out step 5.

This is the worksheet version of the Find & Replace Text dialog. It's slightly different when you launch it from within a form.

When Approach has located the final data match, do the following:

Click here

I | Type in the data you want to locate

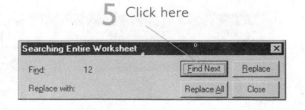

2 Specify the search area

3 Specify search limitations

4 Click here

5 Click here

Find-and-replace operations

When you search for data, you can also – if you want – have Approach replace it with something else.

Running a find-and-replace operation

In a form or worksheet, pull down the Edit menu and click Find & Replace Text. Follow steps 1 and 2 below. Carry out steps 3 and 4, if applicable. Now carry out A OR B below:

A.   Follow step 5. When Approach locates the first search target, carry out step 7 to have it replaced. Approach finds the next instance automatically. Repeat step 7 as often as necessary.

B.   Carry out step 6 to have Approach find *every* target and replace it automatically.

 HANDY TIP

You must be in Browse mode to carry out find-and-replace operations.

This is the worksheet version of the Find & Replace Text dialog. It's slightly different when you launch it from within a form.

 HANDY TIP

When Approach has finished making replacements, do the following:

1 Type in the data you want to locate

2 Type in the replacement data

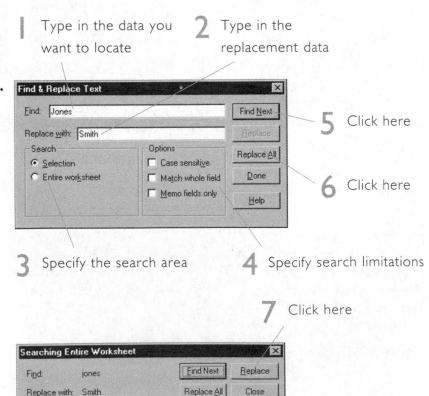

5 Click here

6 Click here

3 Specify the search area

4 Specify search limitations

7 Click here

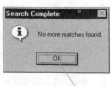

Click here

Page setup – an overview

When you come to print out your database, it's important to ensure the page setup is correct. Luckily, SmartSuite makes this easy.

You can specify:

1.   the paper size;

2.   the page orientation;

3.   the page margins, and;

4.   (in worksheets only) whether or not you want any of the following components printed:

    —   a database title

    —   the current date

    —   page numbers.

With the exception of 4, you can do any of these from within forms or worksheets, but you must be in Design mode.

Note that when you change page setup parameters within a form or worksheet, the changes are not global: they only apply to the original form/worksheet.

Margin settings you can amend are:

•   Top;

•   Bottom;

•   Left, and;

•   Right.

Setting size/orientation options

Approach comes with 17 pre-defined paper types which you can apply to your databases, in either portrait (top-to-bottom) or landscape (sideways-on) orientation.

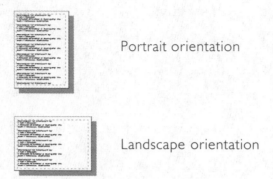

Portrait orientation

Landscape orientation

Applying a new page size/orientation

In Design mode, pull down the File menu and click Page Setup. Now carry out step 1 and/or 2 below. Finally, follow step 3:

Click here; select a page size in the list

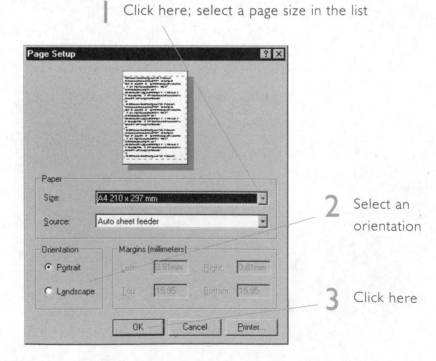

2 Select an orientation

3 Click here

Setting margin options

Approach lets you set a variety of margin settings. The illustration below shows the main ones:

Margin options can only be set from within forms, in Design mode.

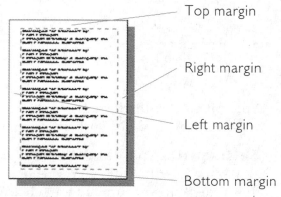

Top margin

Right margin

Left margin

Bottom margin

Applying new margins

In a form within Design mode, make sure no field is selected. Pull down the Form menu and click Form Properties. Do the following:

Ensure this tab is active

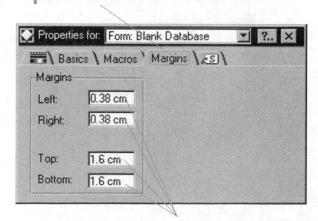

2 Type in new margin settings

Other page setup options

When you print out worksheets, they print as tables or lists. Because of this, Approach lets you:

- print out a heading, if you want, at the head of the page, and;

- include the current date and/or page number at the base of the page (the date appears on the left, the number on the right).

You can specify the heading text on-the-fly (you don't have to insert it within the worksheet itself).

Setting title and date/number options

In a worksheet (in either Browse or Design modes), pull down the Worksheet menu and click Worksheet Properties. Carry out step 1 below, then steps 2–4, as appropriate:

| Ensure this tab is active

2 Click here, then type in the heading you want to use

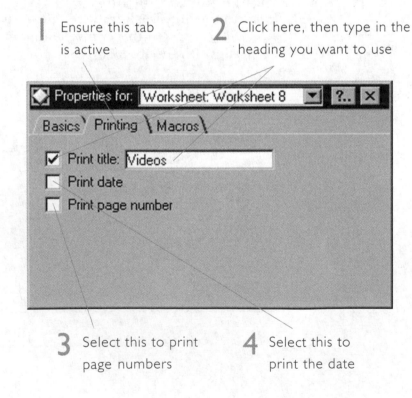

3 Select this to print page numbers

4 Select this to print the date

Print Preview

Approach provides a special view called Print Preview. Print Preview can be launched from within forms or worksheets, in Browse or Design modes, and indicates what your data will look like when printed out.

By default, Print Preview displays your data at a magnification of 85%. You can easily change this if you want by stepping up or down through predetermined zoom levels.

Use Print Preview for a final verification of your database before you print it.

Launching Print Preview

Pull down the File menu and click Print Preview.

Using Print Preview

In Print Preview, the mouse pointer changes to a magnifying glass/mouse (see below):

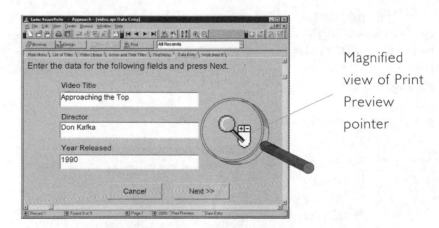

Magnified view of Print Preview pointer

Place the pointer in the appropriate location. Left-click to zoom in (increase the magnification); right-click to zoom out (decrease the magnification). Repeat as often as necessary.

Leaving Print Preview

Pull down the File menu and click Print Preview (the tick against the menu entry disappears).

Printing database data

The available options differ slightly. For instance, in forms (as here), you can choose which records you want printed *and/or* which pages; in worksheets, on the other hand, you can only specify pages.

You can print data from within forms or worksheets, in Browse or Design mode.

You can specify:

* the number of copies you want printed;

* whether you want the copies 'collated'. This is the process whereby Approach prints one full copy at a time. For instance, if you're printing four copies of a 20-page database, Approach prints pages 1–20 of the first copy, followed by pages 1–20 of the second and pages 1–20 of the third, etc;

* which pages or records you want printed, and;

* the printer you want to use (if you have more than one installed on your system).

You can 'mix and match' these, as appropriate.

Starting a print run

If you need to adjust your printer's internal settings before you initiate printing, click Properties. Then refer to your printer's manual.

Open the database/view which contains the data you want to print. Then pull down the File menu and click Print. Do any of steps 1–5. Then carry out step 6 to begin printing:

Click here; choose a printer

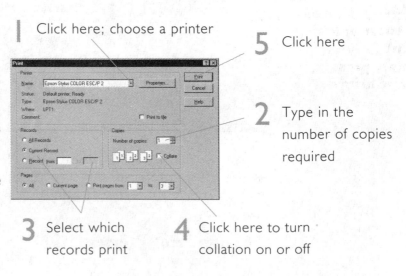

5 Click here

2 Type in the number of copies required

3 Select which records print

4 Click here to turn collation on or off

**Re step 3 – if you're printing a worksheet, select the *pages* which you want to print, instead, in the Print Pages section.
   (If you're printing a form, you can also enter start and end pages in the Pages section.)**

Freelance Graphics

Use this chapter to acquire the basics of producing your own slide show. You'll learn to use views to work with slides optimally, and to move through presentations. You'll apply layouts (with text, formatting and pictures) and styles to slides. Finally, you'll preview your presentation, print it, run it and convert it to a Web-based format.

Covers

The Freelance Graphics screen

Below is a detailed illustration of the Freelance Graphics screen.

Title bar   Menu bar   Horizontal ruler

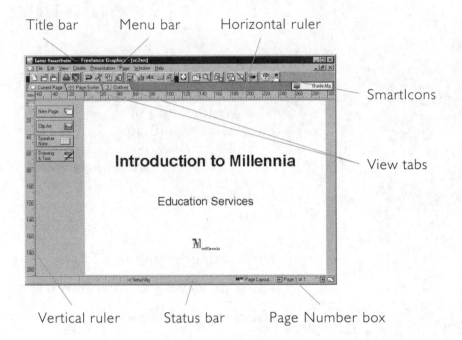

SmartIcons

View tabs

Vertical ruler   Status bar   Page Number box

The rulers can be hidden, if required.

Hiding the rulers

Pull down the View menu and click Set View Preferences. Then do the following:

Deselect this

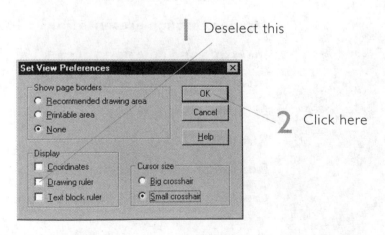

2 Click here

The slide views – an overview

Freelance Graphics has the following views:

Current Page   lets you work graphically with one page of your presentation

Outliner   shows the underlying textual structure of the presentation

Page Sorter   shows all the slides as icons, so you can manipulate them more easily

These are different ways of looking at and interacting with your presentation. The best way to work with presentations is to use a combination of all three, as appropriate.

You can also switch views by clicking the appropriate View tab – see the illustration on p156.

Switching to a view

Pull down the View menu and click Current Page, Outliner or Page Sorter.

Examples of the three views are shown below:

Current Page View

Outliner View

Page Sorter View

Using the slide views

The following are some brief supplementary notes on how best to use the Freelance Graphics views.

Current Page view

Current Page view displays the current slide in its own window. Use this view when you want a detailed picture of a slide – for instance, when you amend any of the slide contents (text or graphics), or when you change the overall formatting or add pages.

To switch from slide to slide, you can press Page Up or Page Down as appropriate. For more information on how to move around in presentations, see pages 164–166.

Outliner view

If you're currently only working with the text in a given presentation, use Outliner view. Outliner view provides an overview of slide structure and content, together with icons representing slides visually.

Outliner has several useful features. For instance, you can opt to have text display with or without formatting (see page 159). You can also print out Outliner text – see pages 173–174.

Page Sorter view

When you delete a slide, Freelance Graphics does not provide a warning message: it's erased immediately.
(You can however reinstate it providing you press Ctrl+Z within 10 editing actions of the deletion.)

In Page Sorter view, slides display as thumbnails. You can use Page Sorter view to perform useful actions on slides. First click a slide to select it (or select more than one by holding down the Shift key as you click them). Then:

To copy the slide(s)	click Duplicate Page in the Page menu
To delete the page(s)	press Delete

To change the size of the thumbnails uniformly, pull down the View menu and click Zoom, In (to increase the magnification) or Zoom, Out (to decrease it).

Restricting slide formatting

In Outliner view, Freelance Graphics displays text formatting and slides display as thumbnails. This means that all formatting enhancements to text display on screen as they would when printed (WYSIWYG – What You See Is What You Get). However, there are times when you won't want this.

HANDY TIP **You can also have slides in Current Page and Page Sorter views display in greyscales: simply press Alt+F9.** **(Repeat to reinstate colour display.)**

In that case, you can:

- have slide thumbnails display in greyscales, rather than colour;

- have slides display as text rather than thumbnails, or;

- display text without formatting.

Customising slide displays

Pull down the View menu and do any of the following:

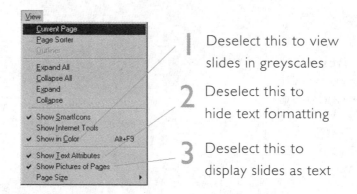

1 Deselect this to view slides in greyscales

2 Deselect this to hide text formatting

3 Deselect this to display slides as text

Outliner view with all formatting deselected

Customising slide structure

If you're using Page Sorter view, select one or more slides before carrying out steps 1–2.

If you're using Current Page view, go to the slide whose layout you want to change (see page 165 for how to do this).

You can customise the basic format of slides very easily in Freelance Graphics by applying new SmartMasters globally. You can choose from almost 50 SmartMaster layouts. When you've done this, you can then amend the individual components if you want (see later topics).

Applying a new layout

Make sure you're in Current Page or Page Sorter view. Pull down the Presentation menu and click Choose a Different SmartMaster Look. Then do the following:

Click a slide format

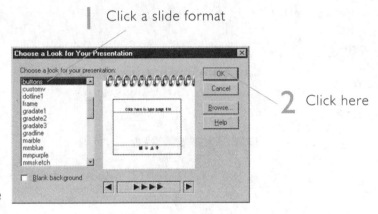

2 Click here

Often, new layouts are not visible in the Title page (the first slide).

The illustration below shows a slide with a new layout:

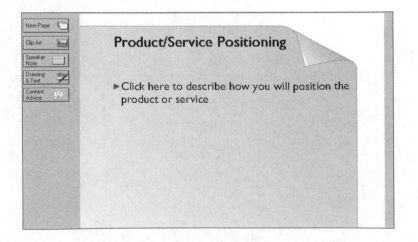

Adding text to slides

See page 17 for how to create a blank slide show, page 19 for how to create one based on a SmartMaster.

When you create a new slide show (unless you choose to create a blank presentation), Freelance Graphics fills each slide with placeholders containing sample text. The idea is that you should replace these with your own text.

The illustration below shows a sample slide before customisation:

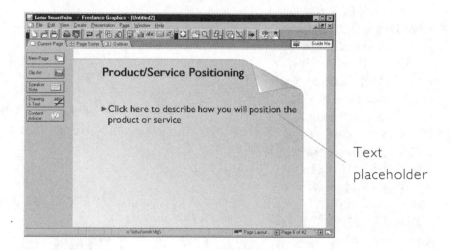

Text placeholder

For help with step 1 (for instance, if you want to know how to start a new line of text), click this button:

A list of tips launches. When you've finished with them, click OK.

To insert your own text, click any text placeholder. Freelance Graphics displays a special text entry box. Now do the following:

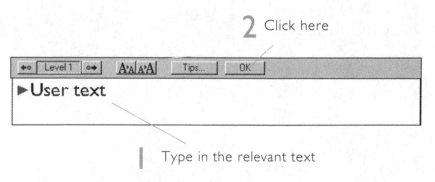

2 Click here

Type in the relevant text

Freelance Graphics inserts the new text.

Formatting text

You can carry out a variety of formatting enhancements on text in slides. These include:

- changing the font and/or type size;

- applying attributes;

- applying a colour;

- specifying the alignment, and;

- specifying the line spacing.

Font-based formatting

Click the relevant text object. Pull down the Text menu and click Text Properties. Carry out step 1 below. Then follow any of steps 2–5, as appropriate (if you follow step 5, also follow 6):

If you want to restrict the changes to specific text within a text object, double-click it. The dedicated text entry box launches. Select the relevant text, then carry out steps 1–6, as appropriate (but note that the Infobox has fewer tabs).
Finally, click OK in the text entry box.

This Infobox is slightly different in SmartSuite 97.

1 | Activate this tab
2 Click a typeface
3 Type in a new point size
4 Click one or more attributes
5 Click here to apply a text colour
6 Click a colour

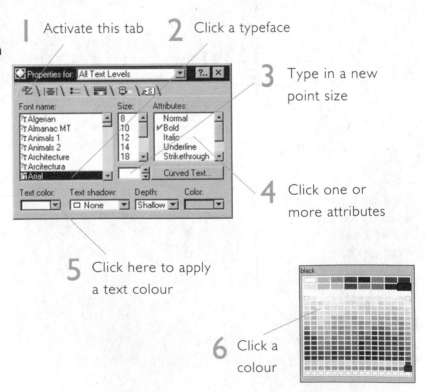

...cont'd

Text objects use styles – collections of associated formatting commands.

To create a style, format a text block appropriately and select it. Pull down the Text menu and click Named Styles, Create. Complete the dialog which launches and click OK.

To apply a style, select the relevant text. Press Alt+Enter. In the Styles tab of the Text Properties Infobox, select a style.

Changing text spacing

First, click the relevant text object. Pull down the Text menu and click Text Properties. Carry out step 1 below. Now carry out steps 2–3, as appropriate:

Activate this tab

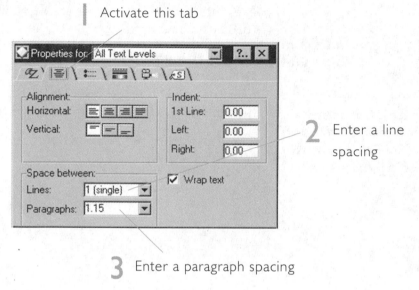

2 Enter a line spacing

3 Enter a paragraph spacing

Changing text alignment

First, click the relevant text object. Pull down the Text menu and do the following:

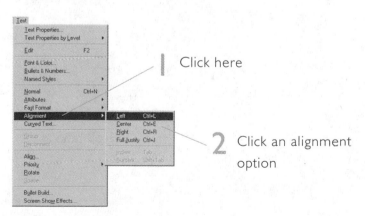

Click here

2 Click an alignment option

Moving through presentations

Since presentations – by their very nature – always have more than one slide, it's essential to be able to move from slide to slide easily (this is even more vital in the case of especially large presentations).

There are various methods you can use to move around in presentations – some work in all views, while others are limited to specific ones.

In Current Page view, the vertical scroll bar merely moves you around the slide currently being displayed.

Using the vertical scroll bar

In Page Sorter or Outliner views, move the mouse pointer over the vertical scroll box. Hold down the left mouse button and drag the box up or down to view other slides.

The illustration below shows the vertical scroll bar in use in Outliner view:

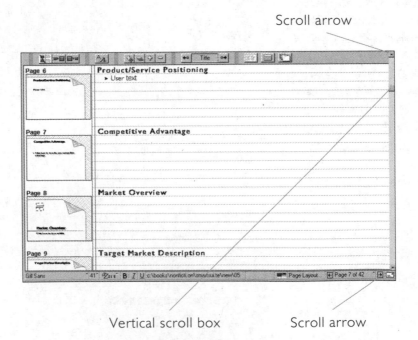

Scroll arrow

Vertical scroll box

Scroll arrow

...cont'd

Using the Page Number box

Using the vertical scroll bar is a fairly inexact way to locate slides. A much more precise way is to use the Page Number box in the Status bar.

Carry out steps 1 or 2 to move to a contiguous slide. Alternatively, perform steps 3–4 to jump to any slide:

See the illustration on page 156 for where to find the Page Number box.

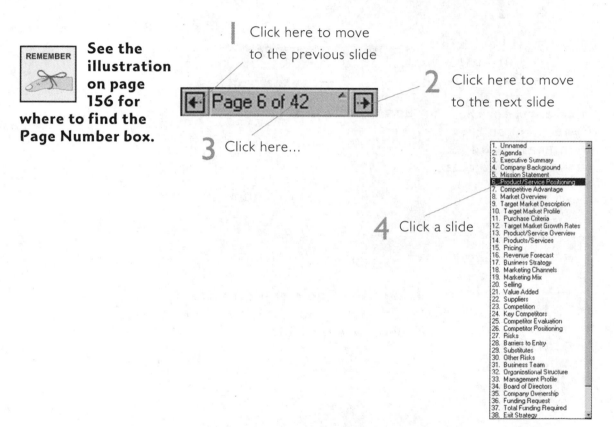

1 Click here to move to the previous slide

2 Click here to move to the next slide

3 Click here...

4 Click a slide

Using Page Sorter view

Page Sorter view offers a useful shortcut which you can use to jump immediately to a specific slide. Simply double-click any slide icon; Freelance Graphics then switches to Current Page view with the slide you selected displayed.

Using the Go To Page dialog

You can use a dialog route from within any view to move to a specific slide.

Pull down the Page menu and click Go to Page. Now do the following:

The current slide is flagged; click another

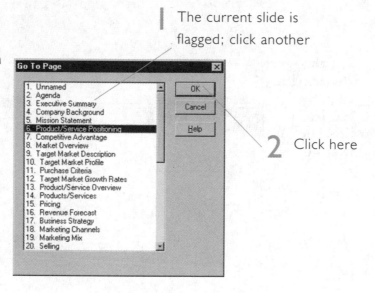

REMEMBER

If you're in Current Page view and there is no entry for the Page menu on the Menu bar, make sure no text objects are selected.

2 Click here

REMEMBER

If you're in Outliner view and there is no entry for the Page menu on the Menu bar, click any thumbnail icon on the left.

Using the Page menu directly

You can also use the Page menu itself to move to the previous or next slide.

Pull down the Page menu and do the following:

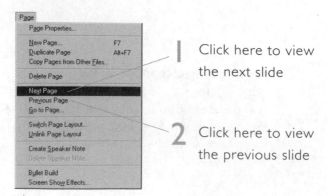

1 Click here to view the next slide

2 Click here to view the previous slide

Inserting and deleting slides

You'll often want to insert a new slide within the body of a presentation. There are also occasions when you'll need to delete a slide because it's no longer required. Freelance Graphics lets you do both easily and conveniently.

If you add a new page in the Outliner view, you can only insert textual components; to add graphics etc., switch to Current Page view.

Inserting a slide

In any view, move to the slide which you want to precede the new one. Then pull down the Create menu and click Page.

Now do the following:

The current slide's Contents page is flagged; click another to apply a new one

Re step 1 – if no Contents pages are associated with your presentation, click the Page Layouts tab instead, then select a layout for your new page. Finally, follow step 2.

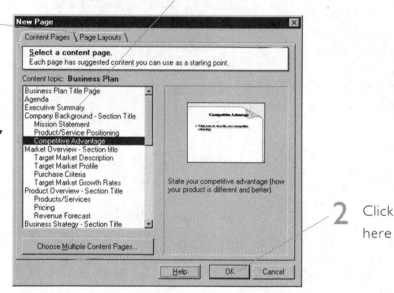

2 Click here

When you delete a slide, Freelance Graphics does not provide a message requiring your confirmation. The slide and its contents are erased immediately.

Deleting a slide

In Current Page view, move to the slide which you want to delete (ensure no objects are selected). In any other view, click its icon (or hold down one Shift key as you click on multiple slide icons to delete more than one). Then pull down the Page menu and click Delete Page.

Inserting pictures

Pictures can help enormously in making your slide shows visually effective. You can add pictures in various ways.

Once inserted into a slide, clip art can be resized and moved in the normal way.

Adding clip art

You can add clip art contained in the SmartSuite Clip Art Gallery. The Gallery stores images in various categories.

In Current Page view, go to the slide into which you want the clip art added. Pull down the Create menu and click Add Clip Art. Now carry out the following steps:

You can also use this dialog to add diagrams. Click Diagram in the View section, then follow steps 1–3.

Click ◀ to view earlier pictures, or ▶ to view later ones. (Doing this also steps through available categories.)

1 Click here; select a category from the list

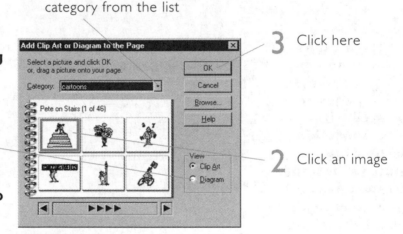

3 Click here

2 Click an image

A slide with an added clip art image:

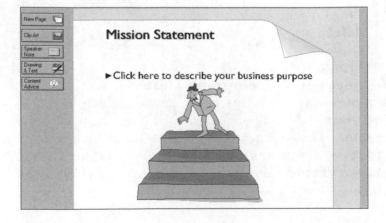

...cont'd

Third party-images can be very useful in slides. They can be:

- output from other programs (eg, drawings and illustrations);

- commercial clip art (eg, bitmap images), or;

- scanned photographs.

Freelance Graphics will happily translate a wide variety of third-party graphics formats.

Adding a third-party picture

To insert a picture produced by another program, do the following. In Current Page view, go to the slide into which you want the picture added. Pull down the File menu and click Open. Now carry out the following steps:

 Once inserted into a slide, pictures can be resized and moved in the normal way.

2 Click here. In the drop-down list, click the drive/folder that hosts the picture

 After step 3, the following message appears:

Click Yes to store a full copy of the picture in your slide show, or No to insert a *linked* copy (this means that the initial graphic file must remain in its original location).

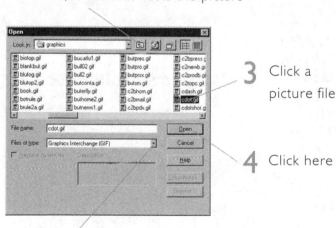

3 Click a picture file

4 Click here

Click here; select a picture format from the list

Freelance Graphics provides another technique for inserting pictures. Some slides come with graphics placeholders:

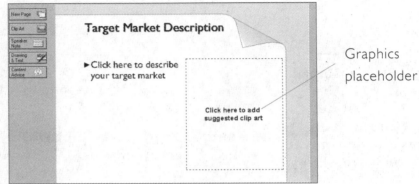

Graphics placeholder

Re step 2 – each placeholder is associated with a specific clip art image; if you don't want to use this, select another.

Inserting pictures via placeholders

Click once within a graphic placeholder. Now do the following:

Click here; select a category from the list

You can also use this dialog to add diagrams. Click Diagram in the View section, then follow steps 1–3.

3 Click here

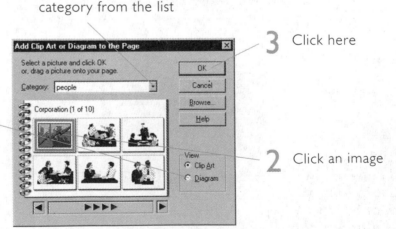

2 Click an image

Click ◄ to view earlier pictures, or ► to view later ones. (Doing this also steps through available categories.)

Print Preview

Freelance Graphics provides a further view called Print Preview. Print Preview can be launched from within any other slide view, and indicates what your presentation will look like when printed out (you might need to do this for a variety of reasons – eg, if you supply handouts with your slide show).

Print Preview displays one full page at a time (even if you eventually opt to print more than one slide on each page).

Launching Print Preview

If you're using the Page Sorter or Outliner views, select the slide you want to preview. If you're using Current Page view, go to the relevant slide. In either case, now pull down the File menu and carry out step 1, followed by 2 or 3. Finally, carry out step 4.

If you're using a black-and-white printer, Print Preview displays your slides as greyscale images; if you're using a colour printer, on the other hand, they display in colour.

To add speaker notes to a slide, select it in Current Page, Page Sorter or Outliner view. Pull down the Create menu and click Speaker Note. In the Speaker Note box, type in the relevant text. Click OK.

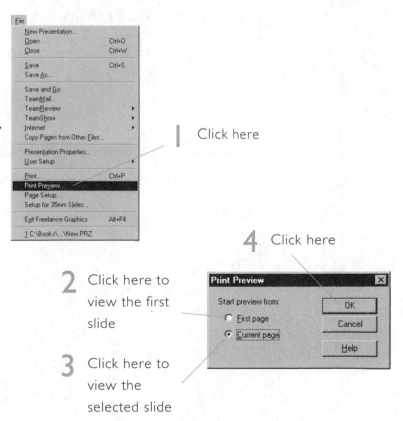

Click here

2 Click here to view the first slide

3 Click here to view the selected slide

4 Click here

Using Print Preview

Your slide in Print Preview will look something like this:

 To leave Print Preview and return to your slide show, click:

HANDY TIP

Quit

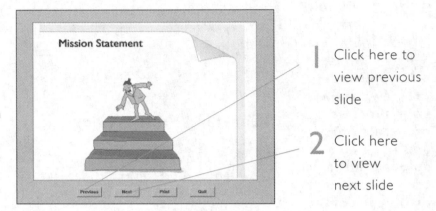

| Click here to view previous slide

2 Click here to view next slide

Moving to slides in Print Preview

Follow steps 1 or 2 above to view adjacent slides. Alternatively, press Esc then do the following:

| The current slide is flagged; click another

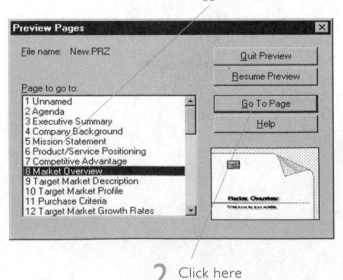

2 Click here

Printing – an overview

Users of the Millennium edition can use another, print-based method to convert slide shows (or any other SmartSuite documents) into a Web format.

Press Ctrl+P. In the Print to: field in the Print dialog, select Net-It Now! SE. (If Net-It Now! SE isn't installed, you'll need to re-run SmartSuite's Installation process.) Click Print.

Complete the dialog which launches, then click Build.

Freelance Graphics makes printing easy. You can specify:

*   which pages are printed (you can specify a range – eg, 3–12 – or print the whole of a presentation);

*   the number of copies;

*   whether you want the copies 'collated' (one full copy printed at a time). For instance, if you're printing three copies of a 10-page presentation, SmartSuite prints pages 1–10 inclusive of the first version, followed by pages 1–10 of the second and pages 1–10 of the third;

*   the print orientation:

 Portrait

 Landscape

*   whether printing is (in effect) in 'Draft' (Freelance Graphics prints no background layouts, and the print time is therefore reduced);

*   whether Freelance Graphics prints your text outline (this option is only available from within the Outliner view);

*   whether your presentation should be printed as a handout, with more than one slide on each page;

*   whether handouts should be printed with blank lines, for annotation ('Audience Notes'), and;

*   which printer you use.

You can also print speaker notes.

To do this, select Speaker notes in the Print section of the Print dialog (see page 174).

Printing a presentation

To print out an outline, first make sure you're in Outliner view. (Then, in step 4, select Outline.)

Pull down the File menu and click Print. Now carry out any of steps 1–6 below, as appropriate (if you follow step 6, also carry out 7 and 8). Finally, follow step 9 to begin printing.

1 Click here; select a printer

9 Click here

6 Click here

Re step 4 – if you click an option apart from Full Page or Outline, select a layout in this section:

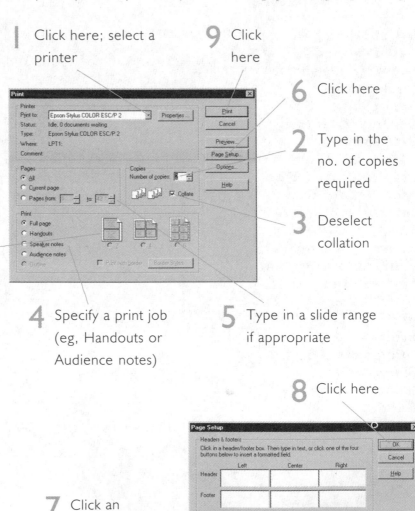

2 Type in the no. of copies required

3 Deselect collation

4 Specify a print job (eg, Handouts or Audience notes)

5 Type in a slide range if appropriate

8 Click here

To print in Draft, click the Options button. Then do the following

Click here

7 Click an orientation

Finally, click OK, then follow the other steps on the right, as appropriate.

Running a presentation

Before you actually run your slide show, it's a good idea to 'rehearse' it (see page 176). This is a dummy run during which you can verify whether the presentation is performing as it should.

Once you've created (and possibly printed) your slide show, it's time to run it. Before you do so, however, you should set the run parameters.

When you run your presentation you can, if you want, have Freelance Graphics wait for your command before moving from slide to slide. This is useful if you anticipate being interrupted during the presentation. You retain full control over delivery. Alternatively, you can have the slide show run automatically.

You can also specify a common transition effect. Transition effects make the intervals between slides more dramatic, and therefore enhance the overall visual impact of your presentations.

Preparing to run your slide show

First, open the presentation you want to run. Then (in any view except Outliner) pull down the Presentation menu and click Set Up Screen Show. Now follow steps 1–4 below, as appropriate:

Re step 2 – if you want to manually trigger new slides when you run your slide show, click 'On click or keypress' instead. Follow steps 1–2 on page 176. The rehearsal begins. Left-click to launch successive slides. Continue to the end of your show, then follow step 3 on page 177.
  When you run your show (see page 177), left-click to launch each new slide.

Ensure this is selected

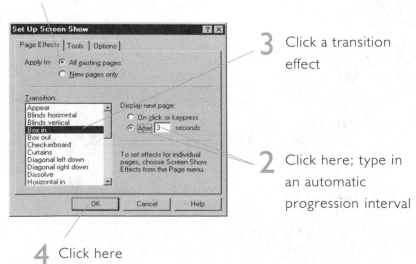

3 Click a transition effect

2 Click here; type in an automatic progression interval

4 Click here

Rehearsing your presentation

In any view, pull down the Presentation menu and click Rehearse, Start. Do the following:

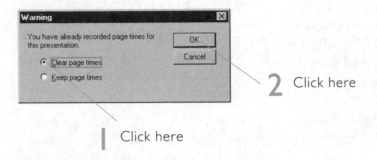

2 Click here

Click here

Freelance Graphics now launches the first slide of your presentation:

If you want to pause any slide, click this button in the Timer:

Click Continue to resume the rehearsal.

If you opted for manual slide progression (see the HANDY TIP on page 175), left-click to launch successive slides.

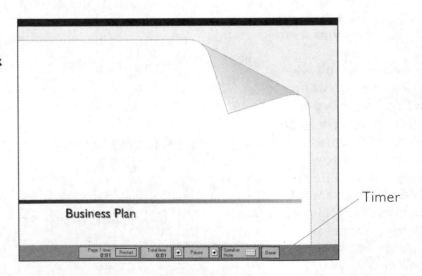

Timer

Successive slides launch after the interval you set in step 2 on page 175.

When all the slides have displayed, a special dialog launches. Do the following:

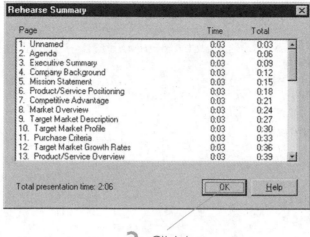

3 Click here

If you need to terminate your slide show before it's finished, press Esc. In the Screen Show Pages dialog, click Quit Screen Show.

If you opted for manual slide succession (see the HANDY TIP on page 175), left-click to advance the slides.

Running your presentation

Pull down the Presentation menu and click Run Screen Show, From Beginning. The first slide launches:

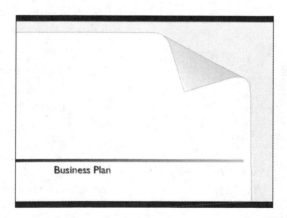

Successive slides display after their respective intervals until the presentation is complete.

Creating Web-based presentations

You can save slide shows to floppy disks for transmission to other users – you can even do this so that people who don't have Freelance Graphics can run them.

Pull down the File menu and click Save and Go. Complete the dialogs which launch (in particular, opt to include the Mobile Screen Show Player if the recipient doesn't have Freelance Graphics).

The remaining wizard dialogs help you:

• set layout options;

• specify graphics formats and resolutions (try 800 x 600), and;

• test your slide show in your browser.

We saw on page 22 that Freelance Graphics has a special wizard which helps you export slide shows to Web-based formats. Here, we'll look at this in more detail.

Exporting to a Web-based format

Pull down the File menu and click Internet, Convert to Web Pages. Complete the self-explanatory dialogs which launch. In particular, though, bear the following in mind:

The second dialog you encounter offers the following choices:

Single Image	each slide is saved as a separate graphics image on a separate Web page. People viewing the show on the Web will be able to see each page one at a time, and in any order.
Tiled Background	as the above, but each slide is broken down into its constituent parts (background, text, etc.). Use this if your slides are largely text-based and don't use many colours.
Screen Show with Plug-In	your slide show is saved as one large file. Viewers can't change the slide order. However, disadvantages include:

• viewers must download the entire file before they can start to view it;

• they must also download a browser plug-in (a one-off operation).

Screen Show with ActiveX	as above, but no plug-in is required. Instead, browsers with ActiveX support built in (eg, Internet Explorer) can automatically view the show.

Organizer

Use this chapter to organise your business and personal life. You'll learn how to enter/track appointments in the Calendar, then perform appointment housekeeping. You'll also have Organizer remind you when appointments are due. You'll enter tasks in the To Do section, contact details in the Address section, events in the Planner, recurring events in the Anniversary section and notes in the Notepad. Finally, you'll link your Calendar and To Do sections with the appropriate SmartCenter drawers, so that entering appointments and contacts there automatically inserts them into your Organizer file.

Covers

Organizer – an overview

To print any Organizer section, go to it. Press Ctrl+P. In the Print dialog, choose:

• a layout;

• a paper size, and;

• the number of copies.

Click OK.

You can use Organizer to:

• track appointments in the Calendar section (and set alarms which remind you of important appointments/events);

• track tasks in the To Do section;

• track contact details in the Address section;

• insert and keep track of helpful notes in the Notepad section;

• schedule meetings in the Planner section, and;

• store important dates in the Anniversary section.

The Organizer screen

Here, the Calendar section is displaying. Most of the other sections are similar in design.

If you've followed the procedures set out in the REMEMBER tip on page 30, appointments you enter into the SmartCenter Calendar drawer are automatically entered into your Organizer Calendar.

Title bar   Menu bar

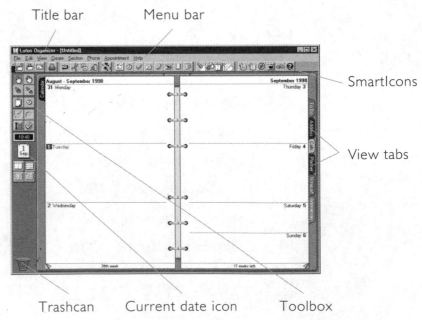

SmartIcons

View tabs

Trashcan   Current date icon   Toolbox

Entering appointments

If the Calendar isn't currently active, click the Calendar View tab.

You can specify how many days the Calendar displays. Right-click in the Calendar. Choose from the following in the shortcut menu:

- Day per Page;
- Work Week;
- Week per Page, or;
- Month.

If you attempt to generate an appointment for a time slot which is already occupied, Organizer launches a warning dialog. Either:

- enter new date/time details, or;
- click OK to schedule the appointment anyway.

In the Calendar, double-click the day for which you want to enter the appointment. Do the following:

1 Type in a date

2 Type in a start time

3 Type in a duration

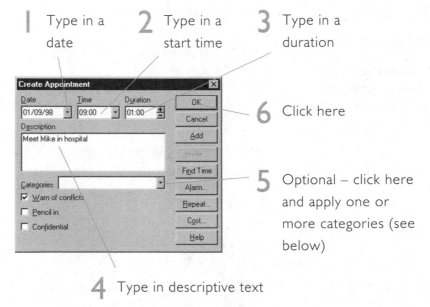

6 Click here

5 Optional – click here and apply one or more categories (see below)

4 Type in descriptive text

Using categories

Organizer lets you classify appointments (and other entries). For example, if you apply a pre-defined category called 'Meetings' to all meetings you set up, you can have Organizer display only those entries associated with the category. You do this by setting up a filter.

Using filters

Pull down the Create menu and click Filters. Click New. In the New Filter dialog, type in a name in the Name field. Complete the Filter section (for help with the syntax, click the Help button). Click OK.

Back in the Filters dialog, highlight your new filter and click Apply.

To remove the filter (and view *all* entries), pull down the Create menu and click Filters. In the Filters dialog, highlight '(None)'. Click OK.

Appointment management

HANDY TIP

To set up an alarm, click this button:

Alarm...

Complete the Alarm dialog. In particular:

- specify how long before or after the appointment the alarm goes off, and;
- specify a message.

Finally, click OK.

REMEMBER

To move to another date, do one of the following:

- to jump to the next or previous page, click either of the turned up corners at the bottom of the page, or;

- to move to another month, click the Calendar View tab. A calendar of the entire year displays. Double-click the new date; Organizer flips to it.

You can perform various actions on appointments you've already set up.

Editing appointments

In the Calendar, double-click an appointment. Carry out steps 1–4, as appropriate. Finally, perform step 5:

1 Type in a new date

2 Type in a new start time

3 Type in a new duration

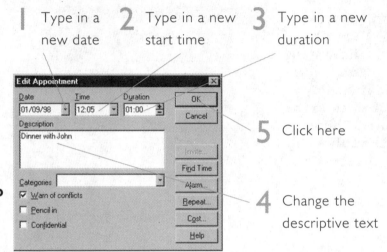

5 Click here

4 Change the descriptive text

Moving appointments

Click this button:

in the Toolbox to the left of the Organizer screen. Click the relevant appointment entry. Now click a new day for the appointment – Organizer inserts it. (See the REMEMBER tip for how to go to another date first).

Deleting appointments

Click an appointment. Drag it onto the Trashcan icon (see the illustration on page 180).

Tracking tasks

If the To Do section isn't currently active, click the To Do View tab.

Creating tasks

Double-click the blank page in the To Do section. Carry out step 1. Perform step 2 if you want to date the task, step 3 to categorise it. Carry out step 4 if you want to rate the task in terms of importance (compared with other tasks). Finally perform step 5:

To mark a task as completed, click this box to the left of the task entry:

1 Enter a description

2 Optional – enter dates

5 Click here

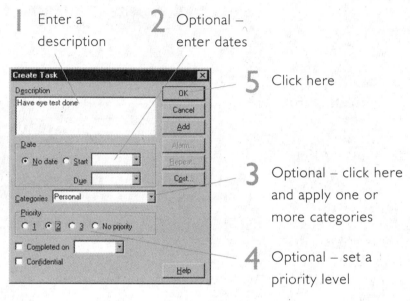

3 Optional – click here and apply one or more categories

4 Optional – set a priority level

Click a page tab to view all tasks associated with it. For example, if entries are being sorted by priority, do the following:

Viewing tasks

Click any of the View icons under the Toolbox:

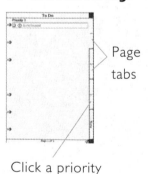

Page tabs

Click a priority

to view all tasks organised under that priority.

 sorts entries by priority

 sorts entries by status (Current, Future, Overdue and Completed)

 sorts entries by start dates

 sorts entries by category

Tracking contacts

If the Address section isn't currently active, click the Address View tab.

HANDY TIP

To search for contacts, press Ctrl+F. In the Find field in the Find dialog, type in search data. Click Find all. Organizer displays a list of all matches in the Occurrences box. Double-click any match; Organizer takes you to the host page.
Lastly, click Close.

REMEMBER

If you've followed the procedures in the REMEMBER tip on page 32, addresses you enter into the SmartCenter Addresses drawer are automatically entered into your Address section.

Adding addresses

Double-click the blank page in the Address section. Carry out the following steps:

Select a tab

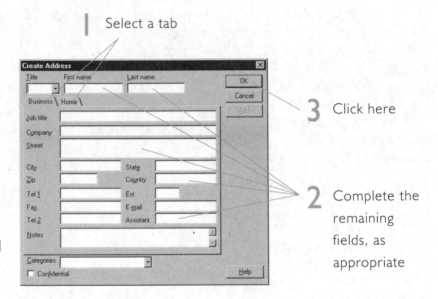

3 Click here

2 Complete the remaining fields, as appropriate

Viewing contact details

Click any of the View icons under the Toolbox:

 displays each contact in its own page

 displays entries by address

 displays entries by contact

 displays entries by phone

Using the Planner

If the Planner section isn't currently active, **click the Planner View tab.**

You can use the Planner to track events which take place over more than one day (eg, business trips, holidays and conferences).

Creating an event
Do the following:

You can 'fold up' the Planner (display it as a notebook). Simply **click this icon:**

in the top right-hand corner of the Planner page.

1 Double-click the day you want the event to start on

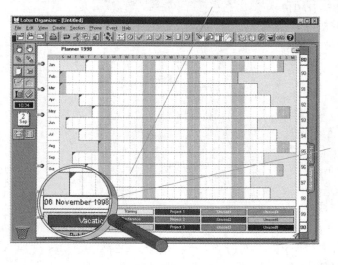

As you move the pointer over the page, the date shows here

To set up an alarm, click this button:

Alarm...

Complete the Alarm dialog. In particular:

- specify how long before or after the event the alarm goes off, and;

- specify a message.

Finally, click OK.

2 Click here; select an event type

5 Click here

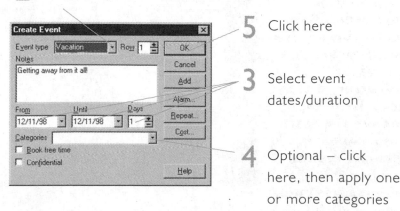

3 Select event dates/duration

4 Optional – click here, then apply one or more categories

Using the Notepad

If the Notepad isn't currently active, click the Notepad View tab.

Use Organizer's Notepad to enter notes and messages.

Creating notes

Double-click the blank page in the Notepad section. Do the following:

Name the new page

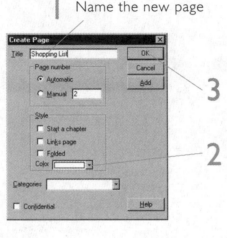

3 Click here

2 Optional – click here and apply one or more categories

Re step 1 – creating a note is a two-stage process which involves:

1. creating a blank page (Organizer updates the 'Notepad Contents' page at the front), and;

2. typing in your note.

4 Click once. Click again, then type in your note

To track recurring dates, go to the Anniversary section (by clicking the Anniversary View tab). Double-click a month; complete the Create Anniversary dialog (click Alarm – and complete the extra dialog – to have Organizer remind you when the anniversary is due). Finally, click OK.

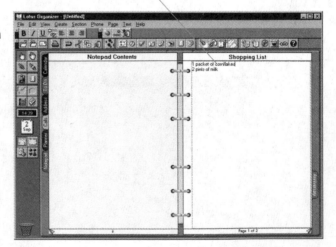

Index

Z